SLAVES OF THE DEATH SPIDERS

And Other Essays on Fantastic Literature

by

Brian Stableford

The Borgo Press
An Imprint of Wildside Press

MMVII

*I.O. Evans Studies in the Philosophy
and Criticism of Literature*
ISSN 0271-9061

Number Thirty-Seven

Library of Congress Cataloging in Publication Data:

Stableford, Brian M.
    Slaves of the death spiders and other essays on fantastic literature / by
Brian Stableford.
        p. cm. — (I.O. Evans studies in the philosophy & criticism of litera-
ture, ISSN 0271-9061 ; no. 37)
    Includes bibliographical references and index.
    ISBN 0-8095-0910-5 (cloth). – ISBN 0-8095-1910-0 (pbk.)
    1. Fantastic literature, English—History and criticism. 2. Fantastic lit-
erature, American—History and criticism. 3. Science fiction—History
and criticism. I. Title. II. Series.
PR408.F34S73 2007   98-31440
823'.0876209—dc 21   CIP

FIRST EDITION

CONTENTS

Introduction 5

1. Slaves of the Death Spiders: Colin Wilson and
   Existentialist Science Fiction..9
2. Is There No Balm in Gilead? The Woeful Prophecies
   Of Margaret Atwood's *The Handmaid's Tale* 19
3. A Few More Crocodile Tears?......................................27
4. The Adventures of *Lord Horror* Across the Media
   Landscape 43
5. Filling in the Middle: Robert Silverberg's *The Queen
   of Springtime* 57
6. Rice's Relapse: *Memnoch the Devil* 67
7. Field of Broken Dreams: Michael Bishop's *Brittle
   Innings* 73
8. The Magic of the Movies..79
9. H. G. Wells and the Discovery of the Future.................95
10. The Many Returns of Dracula....................................121
11. Tarzan's Divided Self 133
12. Sympathy for the Devil: Jacques Cazotte's *The Devil
    in Love*...145
13. The Two Thousand Year Quest: George Viereck's
    Erotic Odyssey...159
14. The Profession of Science Fiction 171

Notes 204
Index..206

INTRODUCTION

The first eight essays in this collection all began life as glorified book reviews. In the first two instances the "glorification" in question was added at the behest of Edward James, the editor of the journal *Foundation*, who had discovered that publishers could be persuaded to pay for *Foundation* to use full-color reproductions of cover paintings as cover illustrations in return for his giving special prominence to "feature reviews" of the books in question. The reason he asked me to do the first such feature review was that it had to be written to a very tight deadline—something that I can reliably do.

The publisher of Colin Wilson's *Spider World: The Tower* apparently had mixed feelings about the publicity value of "Slaves of the Death Spiders: Colin Wilson and Existentialist Science Fiction," which appeared in *Foundation* #38 (Winter 1986/87), but by then I had already been asked to do the second article in the series. "Is There No Balm in Gilead? The Woeful Prophecies of *The Handmaid's Tale*," which appeared in *Foundation* #39 (September 1987) was even less well-received than its predecessor, and I was never asked to do another one, but among the letters it provoked was one from Gwyneth Jones, to which I thought it appropriate to reply at some length. I am indebted to Gwyneth Jones for giving me permission to reproduce her letter herein to provide a bridge between my original review-article and "A Few More Crocodile Tears?," which eventually appeared in *Foundation* #43 (Summer 1988).

The seed of "The Adventures of Lord Horror Across the Media Landscape" was sown by a review I wrote of David Britton's *Lord Horror* for *The New York Review of Science Fiction*. The book was reviewed elsewhere, but most of the

5

other comments were brief and ill-tempered insults whose hostile sentiments were given active expression when the Greater Manchester police seized copies of the book on the grounds that it was obscene. Because I was one of the few people who had actually read the book, I was asked to prepare a further report on it for use in the appeal against the seizure order; the fascinating experience of appearing as a witness for the defense when the appeal was heard prompted me to expand the review and the report into a fuller consideration of the remarkable career of *Lord Horror*. An early version was published in *Other Dimensions* 2 (Fall 1994), the version reprinted here being an updated one prepared for use in an issue of the Meng & Ecker comic book.

The remaining reviews reprinted herein were extended into broader commentaries at my own whim, each of the books in question seeming to me to raise matters worthy of more elaborate discussion than is usual in a review. The review of *The Queen of Springtime* by Robert Silverberg appeared in *Foundation* #47 (Winter 1990). The review of *Memnoch the Devil* by Anne Rice first appeared in *The Penny Dreadfull* 5 (September 1995) before being reprinted, in the slightly expanded version which appears here, in *Necrofile* #19 (1995). The review of *Brittle Innings* by Michael Bishop appeared in *Necrofile* #14 (Fall 1994). "The Magic of the Movies" was written for the *Science Fiction & Fantasy Book Review Annual 1990* edited by Robert A. Collins & Robert Latham, published by Greenwood Press in 1991.

"H. G. Wells and the Discovery of the Future" originated as a talk which I gave to a student society at Imperial College in 1987 (to mark the centenary of Wells's attendance at the college's parent institution, the London School of Normal Science). I repeated the lecture at the 1987 World Science Fiction Convention in Brighton. Since then I have had occasion to give several other talks and write several other articles on Wells, most recently to celebrate the centenary of the publication of *The Time Machine*, and I have taken advantage of the ease with which word-processed documents can be cut and spliced to import some of the fresh meat from the later ventures into the original talk, which was never published.

"The Many Returns of Dracula" was originally published as part of my series of articles on "Yesterday's Bestsellers" after the series had been transferred from *Million: The Magazine About Popular Fiction* to its sister publication *Interzone*. It appeared as "Bram Stoker's Dracula" in *Interzone* #81 (March 1994). "Tarzan's Divided Self" also appeared, in a slightly different version, as part of the same series in a special combined issue of the two magazines: *Million* #5/Interzone #51 (September 1991). It was, however, closely based on the article which I did on "The Tarzan Series" for *The Survey of Modern Fantasy Literature*, edited by Frank Magill, published by the Salem Press in 1983. The present version has been revised in order to correct a significant error which passed unnoticed in the Salem Press essay, but was pointed out by *Million*'s editor, David Pringle, in a footnote to the second published version.

"Sympathy for the Devil" is based on the introduction which I wrote for an edition of *The Devil in Love* published by Dedalus in 1991. The present version is revised.

"The Two Thousand Year Quest" was the last of the "Yesterday's Bestsellers" series, which had no future once the subscribers to *Million* had been paid off in issues of *Interzone*. It appeared in *Interzone* #86 (August 1994).

The final item in the collection was my contribution to a long-running (and still-extending) series of articles in *Foundation*, whose purpose was to give SF writers the opportunity to offer personal accounts of their involvement with the genre. Attempting to analyze one's own eccentric obsessions can be uncomfortable, and one can never escape the suspicion that the "analysis" in question is merely one more neurotic symptom, but it would probably be optimistic to suppose that any of the other inclusions in this collection are any more objective than this one. It was originally published as "The Profession of Science Fiction, 42: A Long and Winding Road" in *Foundation* #50 (Autumn 1991) but my son Leo—the only member of my family to have read it—cruelly suggested that it might have been more appropriately called "A Long and Whining Road," so I have dropped the subtitle. Fans of Douglas Adams will doubtless be disappointed to learn that in this particular instance the number 42 has no significance beyond the fact that the article was the forty-second in the series.

—Brian Stableford
Reading, England

I.

SLAVES OF THE DEATH SPIDERS

COLIN WILSON AND EXISTENTIALIST SCIENCE FICTION

I have before me the proofs of Colin Wilson's new science fiction novel—or part of it anyway, this being only the first volume of a three-decker whose collective title is *Spider World*. Had it been written for the pulp magazines (in a much less prolix fashion, of course) it would probably have been called something slightly more melodramatic, but we live in dignified times nowadays. Instead of a twenty-thousand word first instalment of an *Astounding* serial, *Slaves of the Death Spiders*, we have nearly a hundred and fifty thousand words called *The Tower*, which is presumably to be followed by two more equally weighty tomes.

For the long-time science fiction reader this is a work redolent with echoes; among the works recalled to my mind while I was reading through it were Murray Leinster's "Mad Planet," Edgar Rice Burroughs's *At the Earth's Core*, Manly Wade Wellman's *The Dark Destroyers*, and the film *Star Wars*. Let no one be put off by Colin Wilson's reputation as an unorthodox and mildly esoteric philosopher; this is old-fashioned adventure fiction not so very far upmarket of the recent works of that other unorthodox philosopher L. Ron Hubbard. In the same way that the natural scepticism of the SF fan will lead him to wonder whether there may not be a hint of philosophical propaganda lurking beneath the surface

9

of the ten volume *Invaders Plan*, however, so he will peer suspiciously at the ideative undercurrents of *Spider World*.

The first part of this first volume of Spider World introduces us to Niall, son of Ulf and Siris, brother of Veig, Runa and Mara. (In the great tradition of pulp SF hardly anyone in this world has more than one name, but we will later be surprised to encounter a Wellsian mock-cockney with eight wives who is incongruously called Bill Doggins. Niall also has an uncle called Thorg, but he is just spider fodder). Niall and his family live in the desert, where they must eke out a frugal living while dodging predators and watching for balloon-borne death spiders which might take them as slaves. All the insects and arachnids of this world are much bigger than the ones we know, and some of them are a lot brighter. As well as the death spiders, whose distinctive kind of intelligence is augmented by will-power that can exert physical force, there are sophisticated bombardier beetles which have their own civilization and their own human servants. Human beings are for the most part not as bright as they used to be when they ruled the Earth, mainly because they have been selectively bred by the death spiders for stupidity. Humans living wild, however—like Ulf and his family—are still pretty bright, and Niall soon shows himself to be an intellectual ball of fire, as one would expect of a hero whose ultimate mission will presumably be to save mankind from the yoke of awful servitude.

The cleverness of this small band is amply shown off in the first hundred-and-some pages, when they fight off a series of insectile nasties, domesticate a wasp and some ants, and undertake a dangerous journey to an underground city of free but decadent humans ruled by the surprisingly effete Kazak. Niall, in the course of these adventures, learns enough about his world to give us a rough idea of what it is like, and begins to develop the mental powers that will ultimately equip him to fight back against the spiders. He also finds an artifact left over from the ancient times, which enables him to kill a death spider. This most heinous of crimes precipitates a raid in which his family and the inhabitants of Kazak's city are killed or enslaved. Ulf is numbered among the dead.

10

In the second part of the novel Niall follows the trail of his surviving family-members, hoping to rescue them. He is eventually captured by the wolf spiders—inferior minions of the death spiders—who are herding them into slavery. Their journey takes them across the sea, and during a storm Niall saves the life of one of these wolf spiders, who do not seem to be such awful chaps after all.

Once in the city of the death spiders, Niall finds himself in a peculiar position. The existence of his hidden talents is suspected by the Spider Lord, who refrains from ordering his death in the apparent hope of winning his loyalty and co-operation. This may seem unduly optimistic to the reader, but Niall's experiences in the city show him that the great majority of the spiders' servants think they have a pretty good life, all things considered, and that despite the spiders' habit of eating them their conditions of service are reasonable. They can, at least, feel superior to the utterly stupid slaves. Even Kazak, who has been free, is willing enough to serve his new masters, all the more so when he lands the plum job of being the ultimate overseer. Niall, however, is not tempted.

Niall's determination to oppose the spiders is redoubled when he manages to gain entrance to a tower which the spiders have been trying to destroy for many years. There a computer-generated guru explains to him that man's hegemony was lost long ago when the Earth passed through the tail of a radioactive comet whose effects turned the ecosphere upside down and forced some men to flee the solar system. (This is the info-dump section where Niall is lectured for a while on matters of history, evolution, and so on, but we are not told why all the conventional arguments about the impossibility of giant spiders and insects are wrong.) The computer guru assures Niall that the spiders can be defeated, but coyly refuses to tell him how, spinning him a social Darwinist line about the survival of the fittest and men having to prove themselves worthy of salvation.

In the third part of the story Niall flees the spider city (aided at one point by a grateful wolf spider—not a *cliché* is spurned in this plot) and finally ends up in the city of the bombardier beetles, where he meets, not for the first time,

11

the cheery explosives expert Bill Doggins. Doggins has no particular desire to help him, but Niall has fortunately found out the location of a long-lost arsenal, full of lovely explosives, blasters and other weapons of awful destructive power. This lure is enough to persuade Doggins to put together a crack team of guerillas to get hold of the weapons and let all hell break loose.

The Tower ends, after a brief spider-frying orgy, with the breaking of the treaty between the spiders and the bombardier beetles. Niall is free, but must live as an outcast. His adventure has taught him that the spiders can be opposed, not simply with super-weapons but with the power of the will, and that if humans can only learn to exploit their inner resources they can strike back against their mesmeric masters. Watch out for the next exciting episode!

* * * * * * *

This may seem to be a far cry from *The Outsider*, that rapt commentary on tortured works of literary self-analysis which shot Colin Wilson to fame in the 1950s. It does not even have much in common with Wilson's previous works of SF, which include two Lovecraftian novels, *The Mind Parasites* and *The Philosopher's Stone*, and *The Space Vampires*. The first two come perilously close to sinking beneath the weight of their pseudoscientific discourse, maintaining a deadly intellectual earnestness and a ponderously didactic tone. The third, despite being modelled more on van Vogt than on Lovecraft and being sufficiently similar to the average horror/SF melodrama to make a scary film, still has its fair share of the existentialist pontificating that can be found in Wilson's other murder mysteries, and a certain amount of urgent theorizing derived from his investigation of *The Occult*. Compared with these books, which beg to be taken at least three-quarters seriously, *Spider World* seems to be very much a genre confection, possessed of a more entertaining esprit. Nevertheless, *Spider World* does fit in with the developing pattern of Wilson's work, and it may well be that *The Tower* will prove to be a wolf spider in sheepish clothing; once this three-decker has its reader caught in its seductive

web of melodramatic *cliché* they will suddenly find themselves staring into the beady eyes and slavering palps of that
most hideous of all sciencefictional monsters: the author's
message.

According to his autobiographical reminiscences, Colin
Wilson first fell under the spell of pulp SF when he was ten,[1]
during the war years. He rediscovered it in the 1960s, when
he began to think seriously about all kinds of matters, and he
then concocted an apology for it: SF was the literary voice of
the scientific view of the universe—the grand cosmic perspective—and it was "trying to cure man of his hopeless ad-
diction to the trivial and the obvious."[2] This is, in Wilson's
view, an important task, because it is his own.

What Wilson found in his literary outsiders, in the pages
of Barbusse, Camus, and Hesse, was an agonized attempt to
awake from an awful dream of mundanity and burst the
imaginative horizons confining ordinary, habit-bound, relig-
iously unthinking men. In *The Strength to Dream: Literature
and the Imagination* (1962) Wilson brought together some
very strange bedfellows, chapter one juxtaposing H. P. Lovecraft, W. B. Yeats, Oscar Wilde, and August Strindberg as
collaborators in an "assault on rationality." The realism of
Zola, Faulkner, and Graham Greene, the anti-novels of
Robbe-Grillet and Nathalie Sarraute, the pessimistic avant-
gardism of Beckett, the scientific imagination of Wells and
pulp SF, the fantasies of the Gothic imagination, and the
works of of Hoffmann, Gogol, Tolkien, and Sade are all ex-
amined as flights of the imagination in protest against the
narrowness of everyday perceptions. The different directions
taken by the imagination are said here to reflect the very different values of the writers, but the flight itself implies a
common rejection of the bland acceptance of mundanity. The
exercise of the imagination becomes a kind of groping for
some higher and better purpose in human existence. SF, Wilson claims in this book, is mostly badly-written and cannot
stand up to ordinary methods of literary criticism save in one
or two exceptional cases, but it all has an essential virtue
which no amount of literary incompetence can take away: it
is a spur which urges us to grasp potentials which lie unreal-

ized within us, to become citizens of the cosmos instead of residents of Ruislip.

In later books, most obviously *The Occult* (1971)—blurbed as "A study of the latent power that human beings possess to reach beyond the present"—Wilson informed us that these potentials really do lie within us, and that we might become supermen if only we could get a proper grip on ourselves. Our trouble, he insists, is narrowness of consciousness, which lulls us into "a state of permanent drowsiness, like being half anaesthetised,"[3] in which it is relatively easy to feel frustrated by our inabilities, but difficult actually to do much about it. He promises us, though, that once we understand "the mechanisms of consciousness," and can cultivate the "Factor X" which lies latent there, the universe will really be our oyster.[4]

We have, of course, heard this promise before. L. Ron Hubbard promised it when he invented Dianetics and Scientology. John W. Campbell Jr. promised it during the psi boom of the 1950s, in his lurid editorializing as well as the fiction which he bought for *Astounding/Analog*, and also—it has recently transpired—in the voluminous letters which he wrote to his authors and friends. It is perhaps not surprising, therefore, that we now find in Wilson's work a strategy of popularization very similar to one which has also been employed, in his exploits as writer and messiah, by Hubbard and, in his capacity as editor and agent provocateur, by Campbell.

What has happened to mankind in *Spider World* is a kind of well-deserved fall from grace. We failed to reach our true potential while we had the chance, wasting ourselves in war and luxury, and we paid the price when the miraculous comet gave spiders their chance. Spiders, the plot alleges, already make subconscious use of the psychokinetic power of their tiny wills in directing flies into their webs. Blown up to giant size, their will power is marvellously increased and they easily subdue humans, who have concentrated all their efforts on the cleverness of their hands. Because of this sin, we deserve to be enslaved by the spiders, who are morally entitled to use us as food (it is, after all, merely their nature—although one of the many things the info-dump does

14

not explain is why Wilson's spiders do not need to liquefy their food in the same fashion asthe ones with which we are familiar. The spiders are not all bad—and the bombardier beetles turn out to be scrupulously fair-minded, after their fashion—because the essential patient passivity of their fundamental nature means that they do not generally go in for wars and suchlike.

It is clear even from volume one of this saga that men will release themselves from the yoke of slavery only by cultivating will-power to go with their technological handiness. In so doing they will become whole beings, unlike their old selves or the spiders. The only thing which remains in serious doubt even at this stage is what will happen to the spiders. The pulpish scenario suggests that gung-ho genocide is the outcome to aim at, but we have already seen enough good words put in for them to harbor the suspicion that man and spider might be able to strike a better balance, achieving a symbiosis which transcends the present parasitism.

The way in which Niall's brother Veig initially makes things much easier for the family by domesticating wild insects seems to be preparing the ground for an eventual pluralistic solution by which men, insects and arachnids can combine their different modes of consciousness for the mutual good. The Spider Lord's current resemblance to Ming the Merciless and the Mekon may only be a blind. I must confess that I hope that things will go that way—in these liberal times the reckless speciesism of pulp SF is surely as outdated as its casual sexism—but I remain worried (for one thing, Wilson's sexism is as cavalier as anything one might have found in *Startling Stories*).

* * * * * * *

A cynical observer might suggest that there is a certain irony in what Colin Wilson is trying to do in *Spider World*. In earlier works he joined the ranks of those apologists who could not be content with the condescending judgment that SF consists of "fairy stories for adults who have failed to outgrow fairy stories." When he first began to write SF stories, therefore, he was careful to pack them with lots of heavy stuff suggestive of more respectable literary relationships and existentialist chutzpah. He ran the risk, however, of lending credit to the sceptical argument that all his existentialist woffle and studied support for parapsychology was just part and parcel of the SF bag—*i.e.*, "fairy stories for adults who have failed to outgrow fairy stories."

The will-power of *Spider World* is difficult to see as anything other than the magic power of wishing, and one might easily be prompted to ask whether, if Colin Wilson wants us to take this even half-seriously, we need to take seriously anything else he has ever said. L. Ron Hubbard has surely done much the same thing; while he was invisible to his followers they might just about have been prepared to believe he was a kind of superman, but who in the world could possibly believe that of the hand that penned *Battlefield Earth*?

I have credited these observations to a hypothetical cynical observer because I do not entirely agree with the position. I do not believe that SF consists of fairy stories for people who have not outgrown fairy stories. For that matter, I would not want to be condescending about fairy stories either. I cannot believe, however, that the real merits of science fiction include the ability to tempt us into the development of some mysterious Factor X which will make us all supermen and save us from the possibility of becoming slaves of the death spiders. For this reason, I have mixed feelings about *Spider World*. If I am invited to take it seriously, I simply cannot; it really is too silly. If I am asked not to take it seriously, but only as a mere entertainment, then I will admit that it has a certain rough-hewn charm, like "Mad Planet" or *Star Wars*, but I will persist in regretting that it has very few of the authentic merits which can be found in good SF. It is low on originality, has a sprawling and ungainly plot, and it has not yet extended the horizons of the imagination at all. I still have hopes of the Spider Lord, though, and there may yet prove to be more things in this heaven and earth than I have dreamt of. I have a feeling that we have yet to meet the bees.

* * * * * * *

NOTE (1995): The bibliography of *Spider World* became rather complicated. *The Tower* was split into three books for US publication as a series of "young adult" novels, and was there followed—as it was in the UK—by *The Delta* (1987). According to Wilson's comments in the Third Edition of the St. James Press *Twentieth-Century Science-Fiction Writers*, however, all of this material constituted the first "volume" of the trilogy. A second "volume," entitled *The Magician*, was due to be published in two actual volumes, but only the first of these—consisting of "The Assassins" and "The Living Dead"—seems to have made it into print. It appeared in 1992, under the intended title, from a different publisher. A projected third "volume" called *The New Earth*—intended to consist of three actual volumes—was planned but may not ever see the light of day.

I was never sent review copies of any of the subsequent volumes in the series and I never bothered to buy any of them, so I have no idea how my predictions are working out so far.

SLAVES OF THE DEATH SPIDERS, BY BRIAN STABLEFORD

II.

IS THERE NO BALM IN GILEAD?

THE WOEFUL PROPHECIES OF MARGARET ATWOOD'S *THE HANDMAID'S TALE*

"Behold, listen!" says the prophet Jeremiah (Jer. 8:20-22). "The cry of the daughter of my people from a distant land." Having reproduced her cry, he adds: "For the brokenness of the daughter of my people I am broken; I mourn, dismay has taken hold of me. Is there no balm in Gilead? Is there no physician there? Why then has not the health of the daughter of my people been restored?"

Margaret Atwood's novel *The Handmaid's Tale* is set in the land of Gilead, in the northeastern part of what was formerly the USA, in the not-very-distant future. It has been described as a dystopian novel, but might be better understood as a Jeremiad: a Book of Lamentations.

Alone among the prophets of the Old Testament, Jeremiah mourned—rather extravagantly—his own fate. He complained bitterly of his mistreatment at the hands of those who did not care to hear his message of cursed times to come. Although it is a tale of the future, *The Handmaid's Tale* is not a prophecy in the vulgar sense of being a set of predictions, but it has much of the prophet Jeremiah's urgent and woeful crying. It is fiction and its narrative voice is imagined to emanate from the hypothetical future, thus distancing the text from the real author, so the parallel with Jeremiah is by no means exact, but the lamentations which

19

the story contains are so much the heart of the book that the connection must surely be made—and that story is certainly, from Margaret Atwood's feminist viewpoint, "the cry of the daughter of my people from a distant land."

The reader eventually learns from the text that Gilead is a society which has evolved after a coup by right-wing Fundamentalists. This coup succeeded, in part, because of a state of crisis brought about by a drastic decline in the birthrate. The decline had no single cause, but was the result of a combination of factors, feminist demands for control of their own fertility being supplemented by the catastrophic effects of environmental pollution. The theocratic state has assumed total control of reproduction in the cause of preserving society, using infertile women as expendable slave labor (or, covertly, as prostitutes) while redistributing those who are potentially fertile as "handmaids" who will stand in for barren wives, following a Biblical precedent established in Gen. 30:1-3. Bizarre symbolism requires that the handmaids lie while copulating between the legs of the wives for whom they are intended to serve as surrogates.

All this, however, becomes clear to the reader only by degrees, and some aspects of the Gileadan social order are not explained until an epilogue, which takes the form of a paper written by a historian who wonders about the authenticity of the heroine's taped testimony. In the early pages of the novel we eavesdrop on the protagonist's "re-educated" consciousness, washed almost clean of the pollutions of memory and resistance. Only by degrees is this straitened and bruised mind slowly restored to a state where it can give true vent to its anguish, guiding the heroine into progressive violation of the mores of her new world, until she must escape or be condemned to death. For the reader, this progression is one of gradual enlightenment, both in a factual sense, as we learn more about this crazy society and how it came about, and in a moral sense, as the heroine becomes better able to analyse the horrific texture of its oppressions.

There is an obvious fashion in which *The Handmaid's Tale* can be likened to the classics of dystopian fiction, particularly to Orwell's *Nineteen Eighty-Four*. *Nineteen Eighty-Four* is similarly preoccupied with the policing of thought, the rewriting of sacred texts, and the apparent futility of re-bellion against such intimate oppression. There are some direct echoes of Orwell's world in Gilead—for instance, the way in which the handmaids are provided with a cathartic opportunity to vent their spite in the mutilation and execution of supposed rapists is reminiscent of the ritualized hate sessions of the earlier novel. Above all, however, it is the ironically bitter pessimism of the two texts which links them together.

Orwell offers us a world with no hope left, suggesting that if we want to imagine its future we might think of a boot stamping on the human face eternally. Margaret Atwood is not so brutally direct, but she carefully refuses to tell us whether the black van which comes at the end to take the heroine away is taking her to freedom or to her death. In her historical epilogue, although she allows her historian to make jokes about the excesses and eccentricities of Gileadan society, she deliberately tells us nothing about the politics of his world, save for such oblique satirical hints as are conveyed by the speech which introduces the paper. As the last line of the text signifies, answers to the questions raised therein belong to another province.

Atwood and Orwell are doing much the same thing in declaring that there are trends evident in the contemporary world which, if extrapolated, might lead to tragedy and the magnification of man's inhumanity to man (and woman). Where Atwood differs from Orwell, though, is in her manner of attributing blame. *Nineteen Eighty-Four* is a book about power and control, but Margaret Atwood's narrator wonders at one point whether her story might be about something subtly but crucially different:

> Maybe none of this is about control. Maybe it isn't really about who can own whom, who can do what to whom and get away with it, even as far as death. Maybe it isn't about who can sit and who has to kneel or stand or lie down, legs spread open. Maybe it's about who can do what to whom and be

> forgiven for it. Never tell me it amounts to the
> same thing.[1]

There is nothing forgiving about *Nineteen Eighty-Four*,
but for a feminist work, *The Handmaid's Tale* is surprisingly
easy on its male characters. Even the Commander—who, we
are told in the epilogue, might well be one of the chief archi-
tects of Gilead's social order—is displayed in the narrative
as a pathetic rather than as an evil character. When he uses
his power to command the heroine into violation of the law it
is not (as others assume) for the purposes of perverted lust,
but out of a quieter kind of loneliness. The masculine chauf-
feur, who seems also to be a potentially threatening character
when first introduced, in the end treats the heroine as well as
he can—within the limits of possibility—and she learns to
make use of him even though she cannot love him. In fact,
we hardly see men behaving badly at all, and what we do see
is counterbalanced by images of women behaving badly in
all sorts of ways: the Aunts with their cattle prods whose
task it is to re-educate the handmaids; the moral treason of
the apparently-heroic Moira in accepting a new role as a
whore; the sad deficiencies of the pusillanimous Janine.

Janine is especially interesting, as her sin is to accept the
blame for offences that are not really hers. In the latter pages
of the tale we find the heroine lapsing continually into a
similarly self-effacing, if not actually self-abusing, capitulation with her oppressors. The narrator (unlike the author) is
occasionally in dire danger of losing her moral indignation,
of forgiving. Her view is eventually reinforced by the way
the historians in the epilogue see the injustices of Gilead—as
eccentricities of the historical record, quaintly fascinating,
pregnant with opportunities for witty wordplay. For them,
Gilead is dead and gone, to be understood rather than to be
censured—are we not assured, after all, by another source
that to understand all is to forgive all.

The reader is expected to withhold endorsement from
this view (we have been warned by a prefatory quotation
from Jonathan Swift's *Modest Proposal* not to take the text's
rhetoric entirely at face value) but the fact remains that a key

question in the novel—which we do not find in many dystopian texts—is: how much must we forgive?

It is when we bring this question back from the hypothetical land of Gilead to our own world that we appreciate what an awkward anguish it is that Margaret Atwood's heroine has been made to experience. Her lamentations are inevitably soured by her very generosity; unlike Winston Smith she does not make concessions to her oppressors because she has been taken to Room 101 and shown the most frightful thing in the world. She does so simply because her oppressors are obviously not the most frightful thing in the world, and can be pitied, thanked and respected as well as despised, hated and opposed. There is, clearly, a world of difference between the attitude which a good socialist like Orwell could adopt toward totalitarian manipulators, and the attitude which a good feminist like Margaret Atwood can adopt toward men. One does not have to wonder how much one must forgive a man like O'Brien, but a mere man, unlike a Party member is all too obviously ripe for forgiveness.

In the window-seat of the room in which the handmaid lives during the period covered by her tale there is a cushion embroidered with the word FAITH. It was, presumably, one of a set, but HOPE and CHARITY have gone. That is the way of things in Gilead: faith has indeed been left to hold the field of battle alone; hope and charity are extinct, and in Gilead there is therefore no balm. There remains in this prophetic vision, however, a deeply ironic lament—a bitter-tasting anxiety that the charity of women stands in unfortunate opposition to their hopes. The heroine, in seeking to live in this appalling world, is left without hope very largely because she cannot deny charity to her controllers. Is this, we are tacitly asked, the predicament of the modern feminist? If it is, then it is surely a hard lot, and the feminist prophet can take little enough pleasure from the alarmist warnings which she offers, or from her fragile hope that tragedy might, after all, be averted by moral renewal. For this reason, we find in *The Handmaid's Tale* a tone of voice that is not characteristic of most dystopian writings, and for which we must hunt for other analogues.

"He has besieged me and encompassed me with bitterness and hardship," wailed Jeremiah (Lam. 3: 5-8), "In dark places He has made me dwell, Like those who have long been dead. He has walled me in so that I cannot go out; He has made my chain heavy. Even when I cry out and call for help, He shuts out my prayer." By "He," of course, Jeremiah meant the Lord rather than the male of the species, but in Gilead it comes to the same thing. It always has, and perhaps it always will. *The Handmaid's Tale*, at least, cannot assure us that it will not.

To which one can only add, Amen.

* * * * * * *

The following letter of comment on the above essay appeared in *Foundation* #41. It was (inaccurately) advertised on the contents page as "Gwyneth Jones: Weeping for Stableford."

Dear *Foundation*,

"I weep for you, the walrus said. I deeply sympathise."

The inauguration of the Arthur C. Clarke Award is a great event, and rightly celebrated in No. 39: it is good to know that the whole panel agreed on the literary excellence and power of Margaret Atwood's *The Handmaid's Tale*. However, the "appreciation" of the prize-winning novel provided by Brian Stableford seemed somewhat ambivalent in tone: perhaps not surprisingly so, as feminism in SF is still regarded by some as a controversial topic. Nevertheless, after a detailed description of the conditions maintained by the oppressors and suffered by the oppressed in the fictional world of Gilead—a world which Stableford himself calls "appalling"—it is bemusing to be told that in this book "we hardly see men behaving badly at all." It is as if Atwood is accused of (or commended for) whitewashing the entire Third Reich, on the grounds that she shows a few flashes of humanity in one or two of the guards at the extermination camps. Stableford goes on to express concern at the negative features of Atwood's female characters, apparently feeling that she has fataly weakened her case by showing that slaves are corrupted by slavery, no less than slave-owners. In conclusion, Stableford seems to say that he approves of the book because it demonstrates that women can never get the better of male oppression.

The satirist always walks a narrow line: it is a job that requires enormous delicacy and skill—but not even Dr. Swift himself could circumnavigate Dr. Stableford successfully. Among other disingenuous reservations he fears that the feminist has painted herself into an awful corner by suggesting that the behavior of the men in Gilead can be forgiven: will be forgiven and forgotten, eventually. He contrasts Ms. Atwood's position here unfavorably (from her own point of view, of course) with that of Orwell at the conclusion of *Nineteen Eighty-Four*—Orwell being bold enough to envisage the future as a boot stamping on a human face eternally. To each time the dystopia it can bear: it may be that in the nineteen-eighties writers of futuristic satire live in a perceived world too small and too threatened for the luxury of absolute and nihilistic despair. It may also be that Atwood is a writer of greater subtlety than Orwell—essentially a journalist capable of producing powerful satire, and neither skilled nor profound in his treatment of human character. To tease out the whole "meaning" of *The Handmaid's Tale*, and particularly of the curiously disturbing afterword, in a short "appreciation" would not have been an easy task. But it is clear that Dr. Stableford has been distracted from his job by the circumstance that in this particular warning vision the sufferers from "man's in-humanity" are women--not rain forests, tele-paths, or the ozone layer. The result is a mix-ture of distinctly backhanded compliments, and what seems almost calculated obtuseness. But whatever Dr. Stableford's true position on the question of rights for women—to cattle prod or not to prod—the Arthur C. Clarke Award is supposed to be for a novel with a science fiction theme, not for a writer's politi-cal stance. I can only be thankful that the edi-torial of No. 39 makes clear that the panel of judges as a whole were not similarly affected and that they made their award on the basis of the book's considerable literary merits, as much as on "the relevance of its theme."

Gwyneth Jones

III.

A FEW MORE CROCODILE TEARS?

In *Foundation* #41 Gwyneth Jones remarks upon the ambivalence of my brief appreciation of Margaret Atwood's *The Handmaid's Tale*, which appeared as the "Cover Feature" in Foundation #39. She suggests that the compliments which I pay the book are "backhanded" and that I "seem to say" that I approve of the book "because it demonstrates that women can never get the better of male oppression." She ends her letter by suggesting that whatever the actual intention of my comments was, there remains a sense in which I was "not doing my job" because I wrote about the political ideas which feature in the book rather than its "considerable literary merits."[1]

My representation of *The Handmaid's Tale* as a book of lamentations, although it does not please Gwyneth Jones, has clearly touched some kind of chord, because she begins her letter with a headquote from Lewis Carroll's poem "The Walrus and the Carpenter": "I weep for you, the walrus said. I deeply sympathise." The fact that the editor advertises her letter on the contents page as "Weeping for Stableford" suggests that he, at least, is not sure which of us is supposed to be the walrus, but I am happy to assume that Ms. Jones's attempt to devour my argument is entirely candid in its rapacity, and that the only one who could reasonably be suspected of walrusian hypocrisy is me.

I would like to defend myself against this charge, if I may, not by making any plea of injured innocence (I can hardly ask a court to accept me as a character witness on my own behalf), but by asking some general questions about the addressees of feminist science fiction, and the kind of responses which they might plausibly expected to have, if they are male. I would like to demonstrate, if I can, that there is no possible attitude which a male reviewer could strike which would not lend itself readily to the accusation of hypocrisy. It will be convenient for my case if I can call upon a couple of witnesses, and I will therefore take the liberty of issuing a subpoena to two works which have recently been sent to me for review: Sarah Lefanu's *In the Chinks of the World Machine: Feminism and Science Fiction* (1988), published by The Women's Press; and Anna Livia's SF novel *Bulldozer Rising* (1988), published by Onlywomen Press.

First of all, let me consider the case that the reviewer of a novel has no business placing in the foreground any political rhetoric which it might contain, but should instead focus on its "literary merits."

It is not at all clear whether one could actually characterize a set of "literary merits" which a text might possess apart from its rhetorical content, because even such apparently-basic matters as grammar and vocabulary cannot be considered neutral in terms of content. In respect of feminist works this situation is further complicated by arguments alleging that sexual politics is built into the way we use language. Sarah Lefanu's study of feminist SF refers us to Suzette Haden Elgin's *Native Tongue* (1984) as a novel which discusses the notion of a distinctive "women's language," and one of the topics discussed en passant by the characters in *Bulldozer Rising* is the sexual-political significance of using verb-based descriptions rather than noun-based ones. Given that this argument is stated in the text of Anna Livia's book, it would surely render absurd any attempt to talk about that novel's "style" as if it were a matter independent of its rhetoric. *Bulldozer Rising* does indeed have a distinctive tone of voice, but its author has adopted that tone mainly because it suits what she has to say, not as a mere affectation of artistic individuality. If one is to describe *Bulldozer Rising* as "well-written," then the text itself demands that one should be saying something about the force of its argument rather than any kind of "purely literary" merit.

It would in any case be a fatuous argument which tried to remove the rhetoric of a writer from a consideration of literary merit. Critics only try to do that in respect of writers like D. H. Lawrence, because they recognize that his undeniable oratorical skill is often placed in the service of socio-sexual and psychological theories which are mind-numbing in their stupidity. I cannot imagine that any feminist writer would welcome such a defense, even if she needed one. It is surely the case that feminist fiction is interesting mainly because of what it reveals about the predicament of women in a social world whose every configuration disadvantages them, and that feminist science fiction is interesting because it may have the potential to explore the possibilities which lie beyond those disadvantages. This cannot be made plainer than by the kind of questions which Sarah Lefanu's survey of feminist fiction attempts to address; the back cover blurb (which, given that the author was an editor at the Women's Press while the book was in production, can presumably be taken to have her approval) describes the enterprise thus:

> Can women withstand the weight of misogynist ideas that burdens science fiction and, instead, use its radical and progressive potentialities for their own ends?
> Does science fiction offer certain freedoms to women writers—in terms of form as well as content—unavailable to them in the mainstream?....
> Sarah Lefanu explores these ideas and links them to her thesis that science fiction is the ideal form for the fusion of feminist politics with the imagination...she explores the ways in which feminist ideas have been stealthily at work, subverting male authority in one of its strongholds.[2]

If we can accept that it is the rhetoric of fiction rather than any mere literary prettiness which demands the attention of readers, critics and reviewers, we can progress to the next stage of the argument. This requires us to ask who it is that literary texts address themselves to, and what kinds of responses are possible. In respect of feminist fiction, the first question which arises is whether such texts are, or should be, addressed only to women.

There are some points of evidence which might be brought forward to suggest that this is indeed the case. For one thing, many of them are issued by specialist publishers; the two books which I am using as examples are issued by "The Women's Press" and "Onlywomen Press" respectively (although it should be noted that my possession of the two books implies that neither publisher refuses to send their books out to male reviewers). Then again, the books characteristically offer female central characters, and present an analysis of their difficulties which is clearly of primary interest to readers who are able to associate their own feelings, hopes and predicaments with what is being described.

The argument that feminist fiction is addressed only to females is, however, not so very different from the argument that science fiction is addressed only to scientists. The fact that feminist fiction flourishes mainly within the protective wall of speciality really implies no more than the fact that it is frequently excluded from consideration or downgraded by mass-market publishers. The Onlywomen Press, which labels itself a "Radical Feminist and Lesbian Publisher," is practising protectionist marketing for perfectly sound economic reasons as well as being conscientious in terms of description. The fact that such novels offer female central characters is also less relevant than it may appear; it would be naive in the extreme to suggest that the readability of a literary text depends on the similarity of the central character to the reader (or even to the reader's heroic ideal).

The simple fact of the matter is that insofar as the rhetoric of any literary text touches on matters of injustice or intolerance, then it is relevant to anyone. If a work of fiction intends to dramatize by extrapolation or subversion the sexual-political injustices of our world (or even if it does so accidentally), then it is of interest to everyone. If it intends to be (or is by accident) subversive of the existing social order, or progressive in trying to point out directions of desirable change, then it is equally significant for all parties involved in that social order, whether they are assumed to be trying to maintain it or trying to change it.

This brings us to the real point of the argument, which is to ask whether the response to feminist fiction of male readers is necessarily different from, or necessarily opposed to the response of female readers. This question is, presumably, closely linked to the question of whether men's and women's real interests are necessarily different or necessarily opposed (and if the two questions are not identical that raises interesting questions about the differences between literary experience and lived experience).

It is not too difficult to draw an analogy here between sexual politics and another kind of politics. The writings of Karl Marx suggest that there is a fundamental and objective opposition of the economic interests of the bourgeoisie and the proletariat. Thus, the proletarian reader of Marx, if he (I use "he" consciously and without apology in this particular case) is convinced by Marx's argument, will receive the gift of authentic class consciousness to replace the false consciousness which had previously been foisted upon him by his masters. In contrast, the bourgeois reader, if he is convinced, will realize how very clever the apparatus of oppression from which he has been benefiting really is, and will perceive how much cleverer he might have to be in future in order to preserve that apparatus against the threat of subversion. It is arguable that if Marx was correct in his analysis of the workings of the Capitalist system, the people who benefited most from a better understanding of it were the members of the bourgeoisie who then set out to insulate the system against the implications of its own contradictions.

The situation looks different, though, if we decide that Marx was actually wrong about there being a fundamental and objective opposition of interests. If that were the case, such enlightenment as remained to be derived from his works might be much more homogeneous, with bourgeois and proletarian readers learning more about the logic of a situation which could be altered in both their interests (although not necessarily to the equal advantage of both). It would then become arguable that the world has progressed since Marx's time so as to give everyone's interests a real boost—despite having preserved, in large measure, the inequalities of economic opportunity which were there before—and that further progress might still be made without the actual annihilation of any social group being necessary.

If one were to adopt the view that the interests of men and women are essentially and objectively opposed, one could support the case in either of two ways. One could assert (as some people do) that male and female psychology are fundamentally different, so that they are physiologically programmed to value contradictory things; thus, any relationship between men and women, whether at the individual or collective level, would be bound to involve a power-struggle to determine whose ends are served. On the other hand, one could assert that even though men and women might have identical values if only socialization did not force them into disparate roles, the mere fact that men do have the lion's share of the power leads to such irrevocable corruption that no adjustment is possible save by usurpation. This quasi-Actonian view (power corrupts, but economic power does not corrupt economically!) would direct us to the conclusion that men's interests lie solely in preserving the advantages which the social system gives them, and women's interests solely in arrogating them.

In either of these two cases the male receiver of feminist messages can only be in the same situation as the bourgeois student of Marx—he may learn something to his advantage, but if he does, it will be a very different kind of enlightenment from that which the female writer tries to convey to her female readers. If this is assumed to be the case, then any praising of feminist rhetoric by males cannot help but seem insincere, and any ambivalent comment is bound to seem Machiavellian.

What happens, though, if we do not assume that men's and women's real interests are contradictory?

If one is to avoid the notion of a fundamental and objective opposition, after the fashion of those who try to argue that women's liberation is men's liberation too, then one would have to cast about for a formula for progress in which everyone can get some sort of payoff from a reorganization of society in which inequalities of opportunity are removed or (at least) gradually eroded. The payoff in question might be defined in utilitarian terms or in terms of abstract justice, or both. If such a formula can be offered by the feminist writer, then the male reader of feminist works can receive the same good news as the female reader, and can be glad about it for much the same reasons. Male praise for feminist rhetoric could then be judged sincere, and even ambivalence might be underlaid by real sympathy.

It is interesting to ask what assumptions feminist fiction itself tends to make in respect of the question of male and female interests; and in particular, what assumptions feminist SF tends to adopt.

Not all feminists are alike, of course, and feminist SF comes in several different varieties, as Sarah Lefanu's survey makes clear. Sarah Lefanu also makes clear, though, that there are certain images which are very commonplace in feminist SF—commonplace enough, I think, to be reckoned its nascent *clichés*—which seem to assume a very radical and fundamental opposition of male and female interests.

One such image which crops up frequently is the Utopian society from which men have been excluded, examples of which we find in Charlotte Perkins Gilman's *Herland* (1914), Joanna Russ's accounts of *Whileaway* (1972-75), Suzy McKee Charnas's *Motherlines* (1978), and Sally Miller Gearhart's *The Wanderground* (1980). It is not infrequently the case in feminist SF that when such all-female societies are invaded by men, as in James Tiptree Jr.'s "Houston, Houston, Do You Read?" (1977) or Caroline Forbes's "London Fields" (1985), the threat of disruption is perceived to be so awful that the logic of the situation points inexorably toward extermination of the invaders.

These are not the only Utopian images in feminist SF— the most striking example of a Utopian future which still includes men is to be found in Marge Piercy's *Woman on the Edge of Time* (1976)—nor are they necessarily pictures of perfect worlds, but Sarah Lefanu's survey leaves no doubt that all-female societies are in a very considerable majority where feminist SF's visions of better worlds than ours are concerned.

These Utopian stories exist alongside a whole series of dystopian images, describing future societies in which the oppression of women has intensified very greatly. Key examples can be found in Suzy McKee Charnas's *Walk to the End of the World* (1974) and, of course, Margaret Atwood's *The Handmaid's Tale* (1985); *Bulldozer Rising* also belongs to this group. Such dystopian works as these are not necessarily despairing; although *The Handmaid's Tale* refuses to tell us whether or not the heroine got away, or whether the world has changed for the better, both *Walk to the End of the World* and *Bulldozer Rising* feature eventual escapes by the female characters. It is usually the case, however, that the climactic escape is to an all-female situation, not one in which men and women are going to live together more equally.

These cases, together with like examples, can be held to constitute the heartland of feminist SF (I hesitate to characterize it as a "hard core"). The assumptions adopted within the texts are that the interests of men and women are so fundamentally opposed that no hope of reconciliation can be glimpsed. It is not merely alleged that women can only be free in the absence of men but, as Sarah Lefanu points out in her discussion of Joanna Russ,[3] that women can only be human when there are no men to diminish them. This puts strict limits on the kinds of position in which male readers seem to be placed by the texts.

Sarah Lefanu observes this phenomenon several times in the course of her argument, opining that *The Wanderground* is "a difficult book for men to read,"[4] and quoting Joanna Russ's observations about male hostility to *The Female Man*.[5] Anna Livia's characters are also aware of the difficulty—particularly Ithaca Benaccar, who has tried to chip away from within at the oppressive system which rules and regulates the dystopian future city:

> I invited youngwomen from all walks of life...to write their own stories, sparing no detail. Youngwomen reading these stories felt that the truth was, at last, being told. Now the world would hear how badly treated,

SLAVES OF THE DEATH SPIDERS, BY BRIAN STABLEFORD

> underpaid and unappreciated they were, how
> awful were their lives.... Youngmen, on the
> other hand, read the stories and were pleased
> that youngwomen were indeed being kept
> underfoot, reassured that nothing had changed
> since the last book....
>
> "[Women] felt, and I agreed, that it was
> inappropriate to describe the sort of comfort
> and joy women give each other in books to be
> read in the open market. They thought men
> would enjoy it salaciously; I thought men
> would burn it as sedition. The effect was the
> same: no one wrote of it.[6]

Whether or not in actuality the interests of men and
women are fundamentally opposed and contradictory, the
majority of feminist SF texts do seem to operate from the
hypothesis that they are. If we are to take this at face value,
then the texts themselves determine that the situation of male
readers can only be seen in an unflattering light. They are
refused any attitude except the self-congratulatory, the por-
nographic, or the threatened. It does appear that if a male
reader's sympathies are enlisted for the characters, those
sympathies can only express the hypocritical remorse of the
predator confronting his prey; the texts themselves seem to
insist that any tears a male reader sheds can only be crocodile tears.

If we must take this prejudgment at its face value, what
kind of enthusiasm could a male reader legitimately express
in respect of a work of this kind? Gwyneth Jones apparently
thinks that it would be okay for him to compliment the texts
"literary merits." One might add to this a few other similarly
evasive approaches. It might be acceptable, for instance, for
a male reader to appreciate the wit and humor of such writers
as Josephine Saxton, on the grounds that most of us can see a
joke even if it is directed against ourselves. It might also be
acceptable for the male reader to go along with other political stances taken up in these books, even if they are presented as corollaries to the main argument (one can endorse
a conclusion without necessarily agreeing with the route by

which it has been reached). *Bulldozer Rising* is especially seductive in this respect because it takes up arms not just on behalf of women against men, but also on behalf of the old against the oppressions of the young, and because its city-dystopia partakes of many of the horrors of city-dystopias in general.

If the male critic looking at feminist SF is to talk about these peripheral issues while diplomatically remaining silent about the central theses of the texts which he examines, however, he is surely committing the same folly as the *Country Life* reviewer who remarked of *Lady Chatterley's Lover* that it contained some interesting descriptions of the everyday duties of a gamekeeper but unfortunately kept getting sidetracked into matters of no intrinsic interest. That reviewer was being deliberately silly for ironic effect; it would be foolish to do the same thing in all innocence.

Is there, then, any role which the male critic can play in assessing feminist works? Is there, in fact, any sensible response which texts like these might seek to invoke in the male reader? A simple mea culpa, repenting of the wickedness of the male-volent world, is clearly not enough because on its own it is always going to appear hypocritical, no more than a crocodile tear.

Fortunately, there is one more stage in the critical process which remains open, and that is to move to an actual interrogation of the hypothesis which these texts adopt, which places the male reader in such an awkward position. Is the assumption which these texts make, of a radical and fundamental difference in male and female interests, really to be taken at face value? Does it mean that such a radical and fundamental difference really does exist, or should it be seen as a literary or rhetorical device?

What the intentions of authors are is something that the authors themselves must be left to state, but I do want to argue that the apparent assumption of these texts can be construed as a rhetorical device, and that if it is, it places the male reader in a rather different position from that limited range of standpoints specified by a superficial reading of the texts.

It is important that we do address this question because a naive reading of much feminist fiction (and much feminist SF in particular) might easily lead the female reader straight to despair. If it really were the case that the female imagination, attempting to visualize a better future, could come up with nothing other than an all-female world, then the real-world prospects for the betterment of the female condition would be rather bleak. The disappearance of men is not a likely contingency; nor is it likely that universal consent could ever be obtained for a programme of total female separatism. It is not simply the apparent pessimism of feminist images of future Utopias and Dystopias that is significant here; a great deal of mainstream feminist fiction offers images of unfortunate women so ground down by circumstance that nothing remains for them but madness or suicide.

If this apparently-nihilistic aspect of feminist fiction is taken entirely at face value, then much feminist fiction seems to be saying that there is (unfortunately) no hope at all. Anna Livia makes this point in *Bulldozer Rising* when her heroine speaks sourly of a whole subclass of women's writing:

> Some of them, their spirit's broken before they're born. The books they write, revelling in bruises because it makes them righteous.

Anna Livia is not without a morbid streak of her own, but she knows that there is more to this kind of writing than a lust for martyrdom. Unhappy outcomes in fiction are not necessarily masochistic, nor are "happy" outcomes necessarily hopeful in any meaningful sense—as the feminist critic must recognize when confronted with the works of Barbara Cartland *et al*. This recognition is implicit in the afterword to *The Handmaid's Tale*, where Margaret Atwood carefully toys with the reader's expectations, doggedly refusing to answer his or her curiosity except by deliberately tantalizing and frustrating hints. Writers do not do that sort of thing when they are trying to tell us what the answers are; they do it when they are trying to make us look harder at the questions.

The downbeat thrust of much feminist fiction is, I contend, not intended to point women toward despair, any more than the purpose of Greek tragedy was to spread hopelessness throughout the community. The stories of the present and (hypothetical) future sufferings of women are not intended simply to make readers see the signposts in their everyday experience which make the future threatening, but to make them react to those signposts, to make them question what women are doing and what is being done to them. The same can surely be said about fiction in general, and about science fiction as a genre; the fact that SF deals so frequently and routinely in horrid futures is not evidence of whingeing moral cowardice but evidence that its writers and readers have a questioning temperament rather than a faith-seeking temperament.

The all-female Utopia so often glimpsed in feminist SF is strikingly similar to the male pornotopia which can be glimpsed by riffling through the pages of *Playboy*: what we see, in essence, is a population of healthy, happy women waiting to welcome us. No male thinks seriously about the possibility or desirability of making over the entire world in the image of a fantastic brothel; the Utopia of pornography is not an actual political project, and if we want to understand it as an imaginative device we must look at it in another way. I cannot say how many females there might be whose real political ambitions are to rid the world of men and create *Herland* on Earth, but until I am presented with evidence to the contrary I will rest content with my belief that the image needs to be understood as a literary device, not as a political project.

We need sometimes to be reminded that Thomas More did not wish that he lived in his *Utopia*, and did not want to make England over in its image; what he wanted to do was to use the image of Utopia to make Englishmen think more seriously about the condition of England, to make them question that which they might easily take for granted. We cannot make images of the perfect society in fiction, because we ourselves are the products of a very imperfect society. We could not be happy in a world which reproduced the principles of liberty, equality and fraternity/sorority as fully as any world could, because our own sentimental education has tied our experiences of joy and triumph to other things. The good, alas, are almost as flawed as the world in which they find themselves—the bad are mostly those who have not the saving grace of that "almost."

In this view, the work of serious imaginative fiction can only be either to further and confirm the sentimental education we have already received, or to oppose and weaken it. For myself, I am on the side of the wreckers; the best function of the imagination is surely to make us dissatisfied, to make us ask questions, to create ambivalence where there was self-satisfaction, and in the end to steer us away from the monstrous conclusion that we live in the best of all possible worlds.

This is why I think that it is possible for a male to read feminist fiction without feeling too uncomfortable about the corner into which the text tries to drive him. I do not think that he has to be content with that corner, but nor do I think that he has to come out fighting. I believe that he can come out of it thinking; and that is no bad thing. I even believe that men and women can come to share similar anxieties about the state of the world—and that an anxiety shared is an anxiety squared.

This is why I believe that feminist fiction is not only addressed to women, but to men too. Beneath the surface of the text, readers can reach an imaginative space where that hypothesis about the irreconcilable opposition of interests between men and women is opened to doubt, with the result that we may at least hope that it is false, and that our world might make progress—even though we are simultaneously made to appreciate how hard-won a thing progress always is.

If I am wrong about feminist SF, and it does not have this layer beneath the surface—if its authors really are asserting that the world and its women cannot be saved unless men (not just images of masculinity, or machismo, but men) are obliterated—then I can only apologize to its authors; I have been misreading them, and have mistaken the authenticity of my own sympathies. If I am not wrong, then I am surely secure in the opinion that it does have something to say to me as well as to female readers.

I will await the results of further discussion of the topic with interest.

To return now to Gwyneth Jones's comments on my observations on *The Handmaid's Tale*, I will admit to the ambivalence with which I was charged. I like to be ironic in fact, I take a positive delight in sarcasm, which I know is not to everyone's taste—but I must insist that I do it because I would far rather make a question more pointed than pretend that I know the answer. I am not in favor of cattle-prods for women, but I am in favor of goads intended to coax quiet minds toward the hectic delights of enquiry. However, I am nothing if not inconsistent, and I shall be happy to end this little adventure of the mind with a few uncharacteristically explicit statements.

I think *The Handmaid's Tale* is a good book. It is a good book of lamentations, because it has something to lament. It is a good futuristic fantasy, because it is tantalizing. It asks a good question when it asks how much men deserve the forgiveness of women, and the question is all the better because male and female readers alike are left to ponder it, with only an apparatus of images to place in the loaded balance when we try to weigh it up.

I think *Bulldozer Rising* is a good book too. It is good satire because it puts aspects of our world under the satirical microscope, requiring us to see them in an amended context. It's rhetoric is good because it tries to lend powerful support support a principle of tolerance—a principle which is of importance to each and every one of us, no matter what our sex or sexuality. *Bulldozer Rising* also asks some good questions about the way in which the old tend to lose their human dignity and their human rights along with their sexual desirability, and it makes those questions painful.

To complete the picture, I think *In the Chinks of the World Machine* is a good book as well. It is a good guidebook to feminist SF, because it is reasonably comprehensive and because it reflects an interested viewpoint. It is good because it is more interested in social criticism than any kind of "purified" literary criticism. It is good because it realizes that feminist SF is essentially constructive even when it deals with nowheres and with nastiness.

But have I stopped beating my wife?
Well, what can I say...?

* * * * * * *

NOTE (1995): This article appeared in *Foundation* #43 alongside four further comments by Sarah Lefanu, Jenny Wolmark, Gwyneth Jones, and Colin Greenland as a "Forum" discussion of "Feminism and SF."

SLAVES OF THE DEATH SPIDERS, BY BRIAN STABLEFORD

IV.

THE ADVENTURES OF *LORD HORROR* ACROSS THE MEDIA LANDSCAPE

Lord Horror began life as the eponymous central character of a novel by David Britton, which was eventually published in 1989 although it had been written some years earlier. In the meantime, and subsequently, *Lord Horror* appeared in numerous comic books and also became manifest as a strident if slightly inconsistent vocal presence haunting a number of record releases. If his history is to be properly understood, however, the story must begin some years earlier.

David Britton is co-proprietor with Michael Butterworth of Savoy Books, a publishing company established in the late 1970s. Its early products included a number of previously-unpublished books by Michael Moorcock, new editions of novels by Henry Treece, M. John Harrison, Nik Cohn, and Jack Trevor Story, a number of books on rock music and a few miscellaneous non-fictional oddities. Two erotically-explicit novels by SF writers Charles Platt and Samuel R. Delany (*The Gas* and *Tides of Lust*) were also included in the Savoy list, but the project remained essentially unconnected with Britton's "day job," which consisted (and still consists) of running bookshops whose principal stock-in-trade was soft pornography.

The stock carried by Britton's bookshops was and is of a kind which is generally available in similar shops throughout the British Isles. Such shops are compelled to operate without window displays but are otherwise perfectly legal, even though some of the material they sell sails close to the wind

43

in respect of the Obscene Publications Act, which proscribes material "likely to deprave and corrupt" its readers. Britton's principal shop, however, happens to be in Greater Manchester, which for many years boasted a Chief Constable named James Anderton who was notorious—or famous, depending on one's point of view—for his muscular Christianity and outspoken illiberalism. Anderton formed a local Obscene Publications Squad (the only one in Britain save for the one based in London) to mount a concerted attack on the sale of pornography in his region; in pursuit of this crusade Britton's Manchester shop was regularly raided during the 1980s and various materials were rather indiscriminately seized therefrom—including some of the Savoy Books titles.

Britton's response to this hounding was to issue a plush anthology called *Savoy Dreams* in 1984, co-edited by himself and Michael Butterworth. This included fiction and nonfiction by many Savoy authors intermingled with newspaper clippings, some exhibiting the kind of bizarre horror stories which regularly appear in British tabloid newspapers and others detailing the exploits of James Anderton. The book's chief dedicatee was one-time rock idol P. J. Proby, by then living in alcoholic obscurity in Alderley Edge, and it included a reprinted comic strip drawn by Kris Guidio which featured the Los Angeles band The Cramps. A long article entitled "Savoy Under Siege: A Report from Prison" detailed Anderton's persecution of the company—a persecution which had eventually resulted in Britton's imprisonment. In the late '80s Savoy continued to realize some of the dreams previsioned in this remarkable book. The company diversified into records and comics, although it continued to publish occasional books.

The first Savoy Records release, in 1986, was a twelve-inch single credited to "The Savoy-Hitler Youth Band," featuring Lord Horror on vocals. The record's sleeve featured a caricature of James Anderton, his head exploding amid a tattered halo of hateful obscenities; the lettering on the other side overlaid photographs taken during the liberation of Dachau. The song—which superimposed the lyric of Bruce Springsteen's *Cadillac Ranch* on a version of New Order's *Blue Monday*—was actually sung by P. J. Proby, who subsequently released records with Savoy under his own name. The cover illustration was sufficient to get the record banned, and a new phase in the conflict between Britton and his *bête noire* was joined—a conflict uninterrupted by the subsequent retirement of Anderton.

* * * * * * *

The novel version of *Lord Horror* was issued by Savoy after being rejected by all the leading British publishing houses (Britton, according to his habit, proudly reprinted the ruder rejection slips). It is a complex work which includes among its many characters a chief constable named James Appleton, whose viciously anti-Semitic dialogue is derived by substituting the word "jew" for the word "homosexual" (and various equivalent terms) in public pronouncements which had been made by James Anderton. The members of the Obscene Publications Squad might conceivably have been unaware of this when, on 31 August 1991, they seized 150 copies of the book and 4,000 copies of the earliest Savoy comics (which employ characters from the novel), but seize it they did. Savoy's appeal against that seizure was the first court case concerning the supposed obscenity of a novel since the failure of the British courts to uphold the banning of Hubert Selby's *Last Exit to Brooklyn* in the late 1960s.

The character of *Lord Horror* is (rather remotely) based on William Joyce, who broadcast German propaganda to the British people throughout World War II. Joyce's exaggeratedly plummy English accent encouraged his listeners to refer to him as "Lord Haw-Haw," a joke which quickly became a significant element of the folklore of the war. (The ability to turn an authentically sinister source of anxiety into irreverent comedy is, of course, an important method of psychological defense.) Joyce had lived in England and Ireland for many years before the outbreak of World War II, had been active in Oswald Mosley's Fascist organization, and had fraudulently obtained a British passport, but he was an American citizen and his defection to Germany in 1939 was not, technically, an act of treason. The fact that he was hung by the British in 1946 was a triumph of vengeful ire over more re-

SLAVES OF THE DEATH SPIDERS, BY BRIAN STABLEFORD

fined ideals of justice, which is ironically echoed in the nasty and heavy-handed way in which the creator of *Lord Horror* has been treated by the British criminal justice system.

Britton's *Lord Horror* proudly wears the glamour of Fascism, and exhibits the prejudices and aspirations fundamental to Nazism. This characterization is calculated to excite revulsion and anxiety; the plot of the novel endeavors to achieve its revelations by means of shock tactics. *Lord Horror* is a horror story, an alarmist fantasy, and a provocatively shocking text. The narrative is sometimes very funny and sometimes utterly repulsive, seeking by means of such huge swings of mood to enhance its overall effect. The imagery of the story borrows on the one hand from comic-strip art and on the other from the philosophical *weltanschauung* of Schopenhauer, attempting through such odd juxtapositions to heighten the reader's sense of the awful absurdity of the polite veneer which hides the politics of genocide.

Lord Horror deals with unpleasant subject-matter: race-hatred; the glamour of Fascism; the psychology of oppression and repression. The author's method of dealing with these subjects is one whose roots are to be found in the sarcastic fantasies of the French and English Decadent Movements and in the theatricality of Alfred Jarry's *Ubu-roi*. The novel's central characters—*Lord Horror*, his associate "creep boys" Meng and Ecker, and the Führer of whom they are in search—are gaudy grotesques and their adventures constitute a phantasmagorical black comedy. Their actions, attitudes and aspirations are satirically exaggerated to the point of ludicrous caricature. Britton's Hitler—a quaintly pathetic figure quietly pursuing his research in the philosophy of Schopenhauer while his unheeded masculinity, symbolized by the incredibly expansive Old Shatterhand, entertains extremely inconvenient delusions of grandeur—is not monstrous as a person, but the monstrousness of his career and its legacy are exhibited in no uncertain terms.

* * * * * * *

The first *Lord Horror* comic, also issued in 1989, is something of a patchwork, including several illustrations by

Kris Guidio of scenes from the novel (including one involving "Appleton") as well as a strip-story describing—among other things—the character's encounters with the Cramps and Mikhail Gorbachev. The simultaneously-issued first issue of its companion comic, *Meng & Ecker*, carries on its first page a warning to the effect that "Artistic ideas expressed in these adventures may not coincide with your beliefs—but that's the price you pay for free speech, playmates!" This statement took on an extra dimension of irony when the appeal court which declined to order the destruction of the novel ordered that *Meng & Ecker* #1 was indeed obscene and should be destroyed.

In one of the vignettes contained in this first comic-book collection *Meng and Ecker* drop in on a science fiction convention and offer a brief commentary on the career of L. Ron Hubbard. In another they try to locate Oscar Wilde in Blackpool but fail, although the reader sees him operating a Punch and Judy stall in which one of his puppets is Lord Horror. The puppet Horror displays a "singalong moral code" which begins with a definition of judges as "Men bought and paid for by the state. Will say what they are told. Will kill you to make a point." What effect this had on judge Gerrard Humphries, who confirmed the destruction order, only he can know; it is also possible that he might have been influenced in his decision by the cover illustration, which shows Meng (dressed, as usual, in flamboyant drag) brandishing a knife in one hand and James Anderton's severed head in the other.

Subsequent issues of *Meng & Ecker* (whose 9th issue was released in June 1995) follow much the same unrepentantly gross and somewhat higgledy-piggledy pattern as the first, but the *Lord Horror* series issued alongside them took a very different track. Nos. 3 to 7 (all issued in 1990) constitute a five-part graphic novel called *Hard Core Horror*, subtitled "The Romance of Lord Horror and Jessie Matthews." (Jessie Matthews was a singer and actress who became the principal British matinée idol of the thirties and eventually ended her career by playing the anchor role in the long-running radio soap opera Mrs. Dale's Diary.) This parodic tale of absurdly star-crossed lovers is played out against the background of Mosley's Fascist Movement and the outbreak of World War II, with some interpolated commentary by Horror's brother, James Joyce (also, allegedly, a writer of some note).

The strip story serialized in *Hard Core Horror* features some extraordinarily vivid work by Guidio, which evolved from relatively modest beginnings into displays of an extraordinary quality and intensity. The initially-unfocused strip story is supplemented in its first three parts by similar text stories—which constitute a serial of sorts—printed in white on a black background. In the fourth part, however, the text moves to the front of the book while Guidio's pictures appear in the latter part, mostly as full-page panels without any accompanying text. The war has begun and the imagery of the holocaust has already begun to appear, becoming progressively more horrific, and now the focus of all the text materials becomes much sharper and more intense. In the fifth and final part the holocaust has moved to centre stage, depicted in drawings of a new and distinctive style—which have empty blanks where an accompanying text might have been—and in photographs. A few introductory texts carry information about the actual "Lord Haw Haw," while the single brief textual insertion in the middle of the illustrative material is pertinently extreme. Lord Horror's last appearance, inside the back cover, is as a menacing silhouette; the back cover itself depicts a soberly staring Hitler and carries a quote from Dryden: "To die for faction is a common evil, but to be hanged for nonsense is the Devil."

Like *Lord Horror*, *Hard Core Horror* is a potpourri of the absurd, the irreverent and the horrific, stirred with a certain gleefully-calculated malice, but like the novel the graphic novel has a fundamentally serious purpose, which is ultimately clarified to a much higher degree. It is an accomplished and brilliantly disturbing work of art. Part Three includes, for interested parties, a schematic map of Lord Horror's relationships with other literary works which is not entirely tongue-in-cheek, while the back cover credits describe the various elements, in turn, as "A Savoy Venus and Tannhaüser Production," "A Savoy Gustave Flaubert Production," "A Savoy Ionesco Psychodrama Production," "A Savoy

Deuteronomy Production" and "A Savoy Parallax Production."

The second part of *Hard Core Horror* reprints comments from my 1989 review of the novel which might equally well be applied to the graphic novel, including the judgment that "As intoxicants go, this is bathtub gin toughened up with a strong dose of absolute alcohol—never mind the bouquet, just try to stop your head falling off...it belongs right up there on the top shelf with all the other great works of combatively offensive literature which you would not like your wives and servants to read." When I made that remark (referring to a comment made by the barrister appointed to the task of prosecuting D. H. Lawrence's *Lady Chatterley's Lover* by way of testing the limits of the Obscene Publications Act) I did not realize—indeed, I could not have imagined—that I would end up in court as an "expert witness" attempting to save *Lord Horror* from condemnation under the same act.

* * * * * * *

Lord Horror's career as a recording artist continued with the release in 1990 of a new version of the Cramps' *Garbageman*, credited to "The Savoy Gustave Flaubert Salammbo Orchestra" with Lord Horror—again played with admirable zest by P. J. Proby—as vocalist. The cover art for the 12" single, depicting a crucified Horror, was taken from parts three and four of *Hard Core Horror*. As with the Savoy *Blue Monday*—which is a remarkably effective and shamelessly aggressive dance-track—the arrangement of the *Garbageman* backing track is very striking, commencing with an astonishing drum-roll and proceeding with explosive force.

Garbageman contrasts strongly with the debut single by Meng & Ecker (here impersonated by female vocalists borrowed from Primal Scream and the Happy Mondays), whose A side is the flippantly obscene *Shoot Yer Load*. It also contrasts somewhat with the next Lord Horror release, this time accompanied by "The Savoy King Cocaine Band," which presents a version of Iggy Pop's *Raw Power*. On this occasion Horror's voice was provided by the enthusiastic but eventually-breathless Bobby Thompson; the backing-track again makes extravagantly innovative use of percussion-sounds.

All three of the Lord Horror singles are reprised on the CD album *Savoy Wars*, and are undoubtedly its most impressive tracks. The A side of the Meng & Ecker single is also included, along with several tracks originally released as 12" singles by P. J. Proby and one other item. The one song originally credited to Proby which is peripherally connected with the Lord Horror corpus is *M97002 Hardcore*, a remarkable drum-driven crescendo with a determinedly obscene lyric. The track's title incorporates the number under which Britton served his second prison sentence in 1993—a sentence which followed a series of raids made on his shops after the successful appeal (made in July 1992) against the seizure of *Lord Horror*. Although it would be libellous to suggest that these raids were made in reprisal their timing is certainly suspicious; it might, of course, be similarly inappropriate to state flatly that *M97002 Hardcore* ought to be regarded as a kind of counter-reprisal. The original version contrived to kick up another storm of tabloid controversy by virtue of the sleeve's flippant—and presumably untrue—claim that the female voice echoing Proby's drunken oaths belonged to Madonna.

The odd track out on *Savoy Wars* (also released, in three different versions, on a CD single) is *Reverbstorm*, an original work written by Paul Temple whose upbeat xylophonic dance-track sounds almost poppy enough to be a hit. The lyric is reprinted in *Reverbstorm* #1, the first of a new series of comic books starring Lord Horror, this time mostly drawn by John Coulthart. Four of a projected eight have so far been released (in June 1995).

John Coulthart had earlier supplemented Guidio's work in the unusually restrained and quaintly charming one-off comic-book *Monoshock*, but his work in *Reverbstorm* has grown more phantasmagorically effective with every issue, as he has gradually moved away from modes of depiction inherited from Guidio. An astonishing sequence of full-page illustrations in *Reverbstorm* #4, prefaced by one bearing the legend "Show Me Heaven..." depicts a host of strange monsters—one of which was identified in *Reverbstorm* #1 as "the soul of the Virgin Mary"—involved in acts of violence and extravagant consumption against various industrial cityscapes. These extraordinary works of art are not entirely without parallel in the world of modern comic-book illustration but their extreme grotesquerie also warrants comparison with the works of Bosch and Bruegel, particularly with the latter's visual accounts of the temptation of Saint Anthony—which, via Flaubert and Gustave Moreau, became an important icon of the nineteenth-century Decadent Movements.

Reverbstorm is more of a patchwork than *Hard Core Horror*, but its main connecting thread reunites a noticeably uglier but somewhat less ebullient *Lord Horror* with avatars of Jessie Matthews and James Joyce in a contemporary setting. Each volume so far published follows the precedent set in the later volumes of *Hard Core Horror* of removing the greater part of the text to a separate section, allowing most of the illustrations to stand alone, save for supplementary quotes eclectically plucked from a wide range of sources. The texts vary very markedly, although they all partake of Britton's distinctively surreal style, even more crowded with bizarre juxtapositions than Coulthart's art-work. The text of *Reverbstorm* #4, which deals with the creation of Meng and Ecker by the experimentally-inclined Dr. Mengele, includes a passage which provides a thumbnail sketch of the ideological background of Lord Horror's adventures:

> Fifty years on, Horror had confided to Ecker, Auschwitz would be a recognisable brand name, a mythic character as well known as Sherlock Holmes or Tarzan.... Auschwitz, the holy end-all of life's futile pattern, slinking through the subconscious of humanity, the one archetypal riff common to all nightmares, fuelled on the anvil of Little Richard.... In a hundred years, Auschwitz would form its own genre and become the most successfully marketed product in the history of the world.... The camps were the ultimate enclosed world, the desired image of

world television, beamed by satellite into
each city, town and village.... Guilt would
never stand in the way of commerce, assured
Horror, his cobra eyes stealing the dark.[1]

* * * * * * *

The opportunity to participate in the appeal against the
Lord Horror destruction order—alongside Michael Moorcock and social psychologist Guy Cumberbatch, both of
whom also gave evidence in favor of the book—was very
welcome, all the more so as I had never been in a court of
law before. It was an interesting experience.

During a trial which took place in 1953, after which six
books by the pseudonymous Hank Janson were condemned
as obscene and ordered to be destroyed under the provisions
of an earlier law, the presiding magistrate became annoyed
with the counsel for the defense because he wanted the
members of the jury to read the books before pronouncing
them obscene; the magistrate thought this an unnecessary
waste of time. My knowledge of this remarkable incident,
and my awareness of the extent to which men of the law respect precedent, helped me to be less astonished when His
Honour Judge Humphries begin the proceedings by inquiring
of the counsel for the defense as to whether it was necessary
that he and the two presiding magistrates should actually
have read the book. Judge Humphries seemed rather annoyed
when defense counsel Geoffrey Robertson, Q.C. suggested—
diplomatically—that he ought not to reject the appeal without first reading the book. (It would, of course, be danger-
ously close to libel were I publicly to entertain the hypothesis that the reason why the court overturned the destruction
order on the book, while upholding it in respect of the comic
book, had less to do with the eloquent arguments of the defense than the confidence with which the three adjudicators
could claim familiarity with the contents of what they so ardently desired to condemn.)

It is, alas, the case that few would-be censors are capable of intelligently reading or viewing that which they wish
to censor. They can count the swear-words or enumerate the

acts of violence, but questions of meaning remain obstinately outside the scope of their enquiry. While giving evidence in the court and observing the behavior of those sitting in judgment I was forcibly struck by the gulf of incomprehension which separated Judge Humphries and his stubbornly silent fellows from the testimony of the witnesses—and, by implication, from the world at large. When Guy Cumberbatch attempted to argue that *Meng & Ecker* #1 was no more obscene or offensive than the best-selling weekly *Viz*, it was obvious that His Honour had never heard of *Viz*. Cumberbatch valiantly attempted to counter this ignorance by producing a copy from his briefcase and offering it for the judge's perusal, but to no avail. (In the Janson appeal, counsel's observation that the titles under consideration were no more obscene than hundreds of others openly on sale in any bookshop or newsagency drew the response from one of the presiding judges that they too obviously ought to be banned. It was the resulting barrage of prosecutions that led to the revision of the law and the introduction of the present Obscene Publications Act.)

It may be worth noting that the publications on sale in virtually every newsagency in the United Kingdom, running no risk of confrontation with the law, include numerous "true crime" periodicals which feed and carry forward a widespread public fascination with serial murder, rape and mutilation, as well as several devoted to weapons technology. It is surely irrational to imagine that imagery of these kinds somehow becomes more dangerous when it is transplanted into a wholly imaginary and highly-stylized context. For the most part, *Hard Core Horror*, *Meng & Ecker*, and *Reverbstorm* do not glamorize violence—to the extent that their imagery is consistent and coherent it implies that violence is horrible and ridiculous—but insofar as *Lord Horror*'s gloating razor-attacks can be considered a kind of glamorization they are surely infinitely less seductive than the ads and features in magazines which celebrate the killing power of weaponry with clinical detail and quasi-masturbatory glee.

The battle to save the comic books from condemnation is still being fought and we can only hope that it is eventually won; it would be no trivial matter were it to be lost. At present, the situation seems to be that all of the Savoy comics remain vulnerable to seizure at the whim of the police, and that most of the Savoy records are overtly or covertly proscribed by many shops. (It hardly needs to be added that they are not to be heard on legally-operated radio stations anywhere in the UK). I understand that when the police were instructed to return the copies of *Lord Horror* seized in the 1991 raid they gave back only six of the 150 copies taken, claiming that the rest had been distributed in connection with the court case. The Savoy Wars have not yet achieved a temporary cease-fire, let alone a permanent peace.

* * * * * * *

The censorious mind works from the assumption that unpleasant things are better hidden away. It presumes that what can be kept out of sight can be kept out of mind, and that this will work to the public good. This is a sad and bad mistake.

The kind of xenophobia which led, in Hitler's Germany, to the the attempted extirpation of those Jews and Slavs unlucky enough to find themselves within the borders of the expanding Reich, is by no means extinct. It is clearly visible in recently re-united Germany, in recently dis-united Yugoslavia, and in the nation which William Joyce unwisely tried to adopt. If books and comic books which rudely, crudely and bravely assault complacency with every sharp-edged rhetorical weapon that comes to hand are to be suppressed, the likelihood of that xenophobia continuing to fester unconfronted and unopposed will surely be increased.

Sometimes, in respect of certain issues, we need to be challenged, to be provoked, to be shocked, and to be horrified. That is what horror fiction—in all media—is supposed to do. David Britton is not a soothing writer; his various works are invariably discomfiting and frequently annoying— that is the reason why, in my view, they are worth defending, and worth searching out.

As William Randolph Hearst once said: "News is what somebody wants to stop you printing; all the rest is ads." In spite of being entirely imaginary, the adventures of *Lord*

Horror are news. Like most news nowadays, they are not good news—but that does not make them bad art; their imagery can be uncomfortable to confront, but that is a virtue rather than a fault.

SLAVES OF THE DEATH SPIDERS, BY BRIAN STABLEFORD

V.

FILLING IN THE MIDDLE

ROBERT SILVERBERG'S
THE QUEEN OF SPRINGTIME

In March 1989 I was fortunate enough to hear Robert Silverberg address the 10th International Conference on the Fantastic in the Arts on the topic of the ways in which contemporary SF writers had become "victims of their own success." His thesis, briefly stated, was that the boom in the SF marketplace, which now allows the top writers to claim very handsome advances from publishers, has made it obligatory for those SF writers who want to maintain the high level of their advances to write for the broadest possible audience. In doing that, they must bear in mind that a large part of that potential audience consists of people who have no prior knowledge of the more sophisticated sciencefictional ideas and their development in other works. This situation, Silverberg argued, is bound to have a profound effect on the way financially-ambitious SF writers go about their work.

There was a time—from the forties to the sixties—when Anglo-American science fiction was largely the preserve of fans who read a great deal of it (and little else). This meant that the SF writers of those days could (and, if they wanted to publish in the leading magazines, must) presume that the hard core of their audience consisted of people who had a rough-and-ready knowledge of what had already been done within the field, and what passed for conventional attitudes to certain notions. The tacit contract into which writers and readers entered assumed that a certain amount of imaginative spadework had already been done in considering the implications of such ideas as humanoid robots, generation starships, time paradoxes, and so on; certain logical problems had already been pointed out, certain possibilities already explored, and all of this could be taken as read. New readers were expected to catch up as fast as they could, and relatively little allowance was made for them.

That phase in the development of SF as a publishing category was inevitably temporary. It could not last forever, and it has now gone. Even if science fiction had remained relatively esoteric, the steady accretion of texts would have made it more and more difficult, as time went by, for beginning readers to catch up with the present state of play. I can testify from experience that a beginning reader in 1962 could—within the space of seven years or so—familiarize himself with all the "classic" texts of the genre while still keeping abreast of most of what was interesting in the work being published at the time. The beginning reader of 1982 had no chance at all of doing that by 1989; there was by then too much science fiction past, and far too much science fiction present, to allow anyone to take in all that was "classic" while keeping track of all that was interesting.

In fact, as Silverberg pointed out, SF did not remain esoteric. Its basic ideas gradually infiltrated general popular culture—a process both reflected and considerably boosted by the success of TV programs like *Star Trek* and films like *Star Wars*. The kind of reader who only reads half a dozen books a year became willing to accommodate the occasional SF book within that select batch, and SF books therefore became hypable as possible bestsellers. *Star Trek* did do a certain amount of "educational" work in introducing to a much wider audience the basic vocabulary of SF ideas, but the bulk of SF's new audience had nevertheless to be treated by the texts which sought to woo them as readers without any substantial resources of understanding—readers to whom everything would have to be explained, and whose imaginative capacity must not be overloaded.

(In actual fact, there are some notable exceptions to this generalization; *Dune*, which elevated Frank Herbert to hand-some-advance status, is perhaps the most obvious example of a book which slowly became a bestseller in spite of its perverse tendency to compromize its own accessibility to a greater degree than its content actually warranted. Such exceptions suggest that naive readers may not be so conscientiously simple-minded as the theory implies. So far as would-be bestselling SF writers are concerned, though, it does not really matter whether the theory is true or not, or whether it has loopholes; it is sufficient that the publishers who have to cough up the big advances believe it, and are prepared to act in accordance with it. By and large, they do believe it, and they do act in accordance with it.)

Silverberg had other observations to make in his speech. He had much to say about the way in which the big book-store chains estimate the likely sales of a book by consulting their computer records of sales of previous works. This, he argued, makes it very difficult for would-be bestselling SF writers to step temporarily out of their marketing category, or to write the occasional difficult and esoteric book just to please themselves. The results of any such *jeu d'esprit* are tabulated, and held against the writers who do this sort of thing when the time comes for orders to be placed for their next (hopeful) best-sellers. These comments were, of course, based on Silverberg's contemplation of the results of his financially-unfortunate venture into the historical novel, *Lord of Darkness*.

Silverberg further noted that publishers had become besotted with the trilogy as a desirable format for publication—mainly because publishing sequels is nowadays the only means of persuading the bookstore chains to re-order titles of which they have sold out. This, he said, poses creative problems for would-be writers of SF bestsellers. Everyone knows that the first part of a trilogy has to be a story of emergence, and everyone knows that the third part has to build up to a consummation, but nobody has any satisfactory theory about what is supposed to happen in the second volume, which cannot do either of these things.

All of this is relevant to a consideration of the content and ambitions of *The Queen of Springtime*, which Silverberg must recently have completed when he made his speech, and the writing of which must still have been very much in his mind. In fact, it is very difficult to account for the substance of the novel unless all these arguments are borne in mind.

The Queen of Springtime appears to be the second volume of a trilogy begun with *At Winter's End*—a trilogy which seemingly represents on Silverberg's part a conscientiously-planned stratagem intended to recover and consolidate the best-seller status which was initially won for him by *Lord Valentine's Castle* (which, thanks to the interpolation of a book of shorter pieces in place of a second volume, was also extended into a sort of "trilogy").

The present story is set after the end of the next major ice age but one, which—like all its predecessors, here assumed to be precipitated by periodic series of cometary strikes—has caused a great wave of extinctions. As in all previous instances, rigorous processes of natural selection have produced a range of new biological types, which are now set for a new period of adaptive radiation. But in this case (as in the immediately-preceding case but no others) the forces of natural selection are not operating alone. Our own interglacial period produced the human species, which was capable of taking steps to preserve its own descendants, and the descendants of many other species, by calculated genetic adaptation. This resulted in the creation during the following interglacial period (the one which the story skips over) of the Great World—an apparently-Utopian era when the earth was shared by six intelligent races living in harmony. For some reason (the question is raised in both *At Winter's End* and *The Queen of Springtime* but left dangling) four of these six species accepted extinction. One other—the Hjjks, a quasi-insectile hive-organized people—survived while making only minimal modifications to it own genetic heritage. The remaining one—the humans, of course!—appear to have done something rather more peculiar; they created a new race, physically similar to their own ancestors but blessed with particular powers of extra-sensory perception, whose members were then deposited in subterranean "cocoons," culturally pre-programmed to emerge when the ice finally retreats.

At Winter's End told the story of the emergence of a tribe of "the People" from their cocoon, detailing the trials and tribulations involved in their first meetings with others of their kind, and in the founding of their first cities. It deals with the personal stress suffered by various members of the tribe as the Old Order must make way for a new—particularly in respect of a schism in which would-be followers of a patriarchal way of life break away from the remainder who are determined to cling (at least for a while) to the idiosyncratic matriarchal society which they maintained in the cocoon. The story has several main characters, but the most central is an unruly boy whose questioning ways would have been disruptive in the cocoon but which become vital to the tribe's survival outside it. It soon becomes clear that he must become the wise man who combines the heritage of traditional knowledge with the lessons of empirical discovery. A major factor in the action of the story is the enigmatic Hjjks, who drive the People out of the partly-preserved Great World city which they initially colonize, and nearly overwhelm their second city before being defeated with the aid of a cache of Great World superweapons which comes conveniently to hand.

The SF connoisseur is likely to find *At Winter's End* unsatisfying in several ways. Much of what happens in it is cliched. The post-disaster scenario is old hat, the only really intriguing feature of it being the Great World which has been and gone—but even that functions in the plot mainly as the source for one *deus ex machina* after another, its relics emitting an unsteady dribble of information into the plot until the time inevitably rolls around for the half-hearted orgy of violence which passes for a climax.

It is bad enough that the sophisticated reader cannot really be interested in all this, but the problem is compounded by the fact that the experienced reader (especially one familiar with Silverberg's entire canon) can see all-too-clearly that the author cannot find it very interesting either. The performance is skillful, and there is something to be admired in the painstaking way in which Silverberg conducts the reader one step at a time through a whole series of imaginative notions without ever losing the narrative drive. *At Winter's End* is a slow book, but not a boring one; it serves its introductory purpose reasonably well—but one cannot help feeling that the author's impatience with some of his own devices weakens what impact they might have had for the naive reader. There comes a time when the People—who have thought themselves human—discover that they are not human at all; but the author is so completely aware of the commonplaceness of the move that he cannot even feign surprise. And there comes, as there must, a climactic battle when the misfit-kid-made-good must save the day with the recently-exhumed superweapons that only he was curious enough to search for; again poor Silverberg finds this so excruciating to propose, and does it in such a cursory and apologetic manner, that one cannot imagine the fresh-faced youth to whom such a plot-device is new and bold getting very much excitement out of it.

For all its failings, though, at least *At Winter's End* had the task of making a beginning to sustain its momentum. *The Queen of Springtime* has no such advantage. It is not a beginning, and it makes no attempt to be an end—so what can one do with the second volume of such a project as this?

In the abstract, of course, more than one answer is possible. Leaving aside those trilogies which are (after the fashion of the granddaddy of them all, *The Lord of the Rings*) just three decker novels split in a more-or-less arbitrary fashion, and those which are likewise really two-part works in which the second part is more-or-less arbitrarily bisected, there are two ways to handle the problem which are commonplace in fantasy fiction. One is to plot out a series of specific goals, so that the attainment of each one in turn provides a climax. The other is the "N-shaped" plot, whereby the first volume ends with a worthy but incomplete victory, which is subsequently cancelled out at the beginning of the next volume (whose climax is victorious only in that it stops a decline to ultimate disaster), so that the achievement of a genuine but final victory requires a third volume. I repeat that these are the conventional devices of fantasy—but this is relevant, because the calculated dilution of ideas which is characteristic of so much best-selling SF often converts the stories into a subspecies of heroic fantasy.

In fact, it is only the conversion of SF into a subspecies of heroic fantasy which generates the agonized question of what to do with the second volume, because in a genuinely sciencefictional trilogy no such problem arises. Fantasy stories tend naturally towards closure; the victory of good over evil which convention demands is actually a process of restoration and recovery, Fantasy is characteristically conservative because it has its Ideal State built into it (hypothetically, at least) from the very beginning, and the task of its heroes is to rescue that Ideal from corrupting disruption. Real SF, by contrast, tends towards openness—the true climax of a science fiction story is some kind of conceptual breakthrough which reveals the limitations of whatever "normality" the characters have embraced, and celebrates its transcendence. A science fiction trilogy has to keep on expanding the perspective of the story—something which is not terribly difficult, especially when the story starts with characters who have an artificially limited viewpoint. Science, unlike magic, keeps on unfolding by virtue of its nature—beyond every new discovery there is another waiting to be made.

The Queen of Springtime does attempt to take some advantage of this inbuilt potential of science-fictional trilogizing. There is much more for the People to learn about the world in which they find themselves, and there are conclusions to which they have already jumped which cry out to be questioned, if not overturned. That is how the new story starts out: an emissary of the hated Hjjks arrives in the People's largest city to raise the suggestion that the Hjjks are, in spite of appearances and understandable prejudices, really nice guys from which the People have much to learn. From there the plot flows fairly steadily (and, for the SF connoisseur, fairly predictably): factions emerge, pro- and anti- the Hjjks; nasty politically-ambitious types work underhandedly to foment a war in order to foster their own private ends; the emissary preaches the gospel of Nest-truth and Queen-love so effectively that his eventual assassination promptly turns him into a Christ-figure. The misfit-kid-made-good of *At Winter's End*, by now a lovable-old-eccentric, must use his knowledge, his cleverness and his magical all-purpose-*cliché*-device to discover the real truth about the Hjjks and sort things out before war destroys everything.

It might have worked, but for two things. The first is that the author cannot really buy it. He has done this sort of thing before, often—and has done it with a passion and an intensity which would be inappropriate in a slow-moving, one-step-at-a-time text like this—and he is all-too-clearly aware that this version of it is a stripped-down finger exercise with no guts. The second is that the author is uncertain as to how far one might dare to go in this direction before losing the goodwill of huge chunks of his audience. In his passionate and intense days, of course, he was uninhibited—he went wherever the force of his logic and the drive of his passion would take him, even if it took him to conclusions which he knew would prove unpopular with many of his readers (*Downward to the Earth, Dying Inside*) or into literary and imaginative territory which he knew would be incomprehensible to many of those readers (*Son of Man*). In those days, he was a bold explorer, not a careful crowd-pleaser—but that was then and this is now.

The result of this uncertainty is a process of prevarication which initially promises to be intriguing, but under the enervating influence of the author's own lack of conviction decays in the end into mere floundering. So when the time comes for the climax, what do we get? Goodbye science fiction, welcome back fantasy. A minor character invented solely for the purpose finds a hole in a hillside, and inside the cave are some relics of the Great World, which turn out to be...SUPERWEAPONS! And lest any innocent reader might think that in view of what has gone before these weapons are too dreadful to use, there's an equally-serendipitous revelation which explains why it's okay to sock it to the Hjjks in spite of everything which has been said in their favor....

I have every confidence that volume three of this particular trilogy will have some good stuff in it. All the interesting questions will then be answered. We will have to be told why the humans did what they did when the time came for the Great World to end—and, for that matter, how the

Great World itself came to be. (I have a strong suspicion that I already know the answers to these questions, but I am willing to be surprised—in fact, I fervently hope that I am surprised.) Then again, the expansion of perspective whose beginnings are plotted out in the sidelines of *The Queen of Springtime*, will eventually have to be brought to long-delayed fruition (keep an eye out for the holier-than-we caviandis!)

In the meantime, *The Queen of Springtime*, viewed as a project in itself, does indeed raise the question of what the hell it is for—and the only answer one can offer is that it exists to fill in that embarrassing gap between emergence and resolution which is created by the publisher's excessive love for the trilogy. It is padding, and its only saving grace is the fact that because the whole project was planned on a no-previous-experience-necessary basis it doesn't entirely waste its generous allocation of word-space; it does, at least, put in its ration of spadework in preparation for the revelations to come.

I loved the works which Robert Silverberg produced in the years he was an intense, passionate, uninhibited writer of sophisticated science fiction. I remember the books which he wrote in that phase of his career with great affection and great admiration, but I can understand why he ultimately came to the end of that phase of his career, why he harbored bitter thoughts for a while when he reflected on some of the consequences which stemmed from it, and why he is now following a markedly different career-plan. I hope that he would understand in his turn why I am disappointed by *The Queen of Springtime*.

* * * * * * *

NOTE (1995): No third volume has yet appeared to continue or complete the "New Springtime" series. I have no idea why.

SLAVES OF THE DEATH SPIDERS, BY BRIAN STABLEFORD

VI.

RICE'S RELAPSE

MEMNOCH THE DEVIL

"If God did not exist," Voltaire once wrote, "it would be necessary to invent Him." He was, of course, being sarcastic; Voltaire knew perfectly well that God did not exist, and that mankind had invented Him. The real question under consideration is: now that we know that God does not exist, can we do away with Him altogether or are we somehow bound by necessity to keep on reinventing Him?

When she began the Vampire Chronicles, Anne Rice seemed to have taken the view that God had become an irrelevance, even to the supposedly-damned. The luckless Louis, suckered into angst-ridden superhumanity in *Interview with the Vampire* (1976), searched in vain for proof of his own condemnation to Hellfire but only managed to inflict punishments upon himself. The second volume of the series—in which Louis's own creator, the charismatic Lestat, began to tell his own story—seemed even more insistent upon this point. The superstitious vampires of eighteenth-century Paris would not enter the Cathedral of Notre Dame lest they be struck down by the wrath of God, but when Lestat put their fear to the test nothing happened. That non-event struck him with all the force of revelation, informing him that he was free to be what Nature had made him: free not merely to kill, but to revel in killing. Lapsed Catholics are always prone to reproduce the absolutist zeal of Catholicism

67

in their new-found atheism—a tendency which bodes ill should they ever be tempted to lapse back again.

Lestat's subsequent researches into his origins and nature, as dutifully recorded by his lapsed Catholic creator, revealed no evidence at all of the existence of God or the Devil. His consequent reappraisal of the inherent amorality of the vampire condition seemed to be utterly secure. This was, one presumes, one of the keys to his extraordinary success in attracting disciples among the reading public, who yearned—as do we all—to be free, at least for for measured intervals in the privacy of the imagination, from the burdens of social and moral conformity. On the other hand, the very fact that the matter kept coming up in the texts was just a trifle suspicious. It was as if the unprovability of the negative conclusion were an itch that—for the author if not the character—simply would not be quieted.

It is, therefore, not entirely surprising that the fifth volume of the Vampire Chronicles marks a sharp change in direction. Here, Lestat finds out that God and the Devil do exist, and that the Devil—who does not like to be called Satan, preferring Memnoch on the grounds that it is his real name— wants to recruit him as a star player for the diabolical team. By way of persuading his chosen appointee to accept his offer, Memnoch takes Lestat to Heaven to meet God and relates his entire life story (with full explanations of his conduct). Memnoch then whips Lestat back in time to witness the crucifixion and takes him to Hell—just for a visit—so that the purpose of that particular project can be made clear. There is a frame narrative of sorts in which this exhaustive account of Creation is embedded, but it exists only to facilitate a further analysis of the nature of the Christian religion, and the significance of the sacred artefacts of Catholicism as a force in human affairs.

What *Memnoch the Devil* amounts to, in effect, is the most sustained exercise in literary Satanism ever to have been carried out. By "literary Satanism" I mean the tradition which is constituted by literary works which have followed up William Blake's remark that Milton, in writing *Paradise Lost*, had been "of the Devil's party without knowing it." Works making up this fascinating tradition have made out a variety of apologetic cases in which the Devil became a heroic rebel rather than an archetype of evil; Anatole France's *The Revolt of the Angels* (1914) remains the subgenre's pinnacle of literary achievement.

This is, of course, unusual territory for bestselling writers; Marie Corelli's *The Sorrows of Satan* (1895) is the only previous venture of this kind by an author possessed of an audience as broad and as numerous as Anne Rice's, and Rice grasps the nettle much more firmly than Marie Corelli did. Indeed, it is arguable that Rice grasps the nettle far more firmly than anyone has ever done before, including Anatole France and John Cowper Powys (whose epic poem *Lucifer*, written in 1905, but not published until 1956, is arguably the most forthright example previously written in English, although William Gerhardi and Brian Lunn's *The Memoirs of Satan*, 1932, might qualify were it not a parody). How brave this decision was in terms of commercial fortune and critical appraisal remains to be seen, but one thing beyond doubt is that it will be a devilishly difficult act for Rice to follow. Now that Lestat has met God and learned everything he could ever want to know about Creation, how can he ever interest himself again in anything as trivial as body-swapping or rock superstardom?

Even Voltaire would have to admit that Rice's reinvention of God is ingenious, and her reinvention of the Devil even more so. She is, of course, standing on the shoulders of giants, but she has taken full advantage of that standpoint. Like Anatole France before her (and riding a wave of current fashionability) she derives her account of the War in Heaven—which here becomes a Philosophical Disagreement in Heaven—from selected passages of the apocryphal Book of Enoch, making the archetypal fallen angel into a Watcher who becomes a little too intimately involved with those he watches. This allows Memnoch to play the Promethean role celebrated by virtually all previous literary Satanists, but Rice adds a cunning twist which allows him to retain both his status as overlord of Hell and the honest respect of his great adversary, God. Rice cleverly interweaves her modified Enochian history into modern conceptions of the history of the earth and the evolution of human societies, and does not shirk the project which most modern writers of religious fantasy have either avoided or rendered silly: the description of Heaven. Even Voltaire would have to admit, in fact, that Memnoch the Devil is a fascinating and engaging book.

Having admitted all this, though, Voltaire would surely have gone on to observe that however brilliantly *Memnoch the Devil* is put together, there remains something vitally important that has been left out. Rice's God has indeed been thoroughly reinvented, but His Creation remains as stubbornly geocentric and anthropocentric as anything envisaged in pre-Copernican days. In order to restore the relevance of God, Rice is forced to declare the universe beyond the earth irrelevant (and Memnoch explicitly does so at an early point in his discourse). Not all reinventions of God are forced to this extreme—Olaf Stapledon's *Star Maker* (1937) is a conspicuous exception—but ones which work within a specifically Christian framework, let alone a specifically Catholic one, are bound to make human beings the linch-pin of their argument. The Christian God, like His immediate antecedents, was invented in order to create humankind, and his adversary the Devil was invented to plague humankind; whatever their argument was initially about, humankind was and must remain their battleground. While that remains the case, the rich, complex and vast universe of modern science will always constitute glaring evidence to the effect that what we are dealing with when we confront such visions is not merely an invention but an invention whose necessity is way past its sell-by date.

It must not be forgotten, of course, that the account of God, Creation, and the Devil which is contained in *Memnoch the Devil* is not the only reinvention which requires consideration here. The narrator who is granted this vision is also a reinvention; his attitude is not that of an ordinary man but that of a vampire, and a very specific kind of vampire at that. Lestat's earlier adventures have also been, in their humble way, exercises in literary Satanism. They too have taken a figure previously used as an archetype of evil and have subjected his attributes to ingenious apologetic reappraisal. By necessity, Lestat views the history of humankind not as a human but as an unrepentant predator upon humanity, who has always previously taken the argumentative line that if he is damned, he will be proudly and defiantly damned.

Actually, and puzzlingly, Lestat tells us in the prologue to his story that "it doesn't matter here that I'm a vampire. It is not central to the tale." This is, if taken at face value, an astonishing claim, tantamount to a confession that the author has framed her account of Creation as an episode of the vampire chronicles purely and simply as a means of selling it to a public which has every right to expect something much more akin to *The Tale of the Body Thief* (1992). It also lends a particular awkwardness to the thorny question of why Memnoch wants so desperately to recruit Lestat—another matter which, in the end, Rice shirks, not by brazenly declaring it irrelevant but by cravenly rendering it deeply and inextricably problematic. Memnoch's account of Creation and its dynamics does provide an explanation of what vampires are and how they came into being, but it does so as a quirky aside and Lestat hardly reacts at all to the revelation, his mind by then being intent on larger matters.

Whatever Rice intended, however, the reader of the book, in stepping imaginatively into Lestat's shoes, is able to see the story from the distanced viewpoint of a defiantly unhuman petty Satan—and the fact that the reader can do that (and surely should) makes a difference. The difference it makes is, I think, crucial to the dilemma in which Lestat is placed when he meets God and God expresses the polite hope that Lestat will never be his adversary. The reader-as-Lestat might well react to this incident in a spirit rather less humble than the one in which the author-as-Lestat does, thus being thrown into a rather uncomfortable relationship with the remainder of the text.

Like Marie Corelli before her—but unlike Blake, Shelley, Baudelaire, Anatole France, and the other central figures of the Great Tradition of Literary Satanism—Anne Rice wants to make an apologetic case for the Devil without insulting, or even offending, God. She wants to make all the world's sufferings morally explicable in a way which will allow God to retain His Divine Right to stand idly by. Because Rice wants to do that—perhaps because of some recent reconciliation with the faith of her childhood—Memnoch wants to do it too, and so, at least for the duration of this particular text, does Lestat. The reader of Lestat's previous adventures will know, however, that Lestat is acting way out of character here. Any connoisseur of modern vampire fiction will know full well that Lestat the vampire would take the view, even if *Memnoch the Devil* did not, that God's argument simply won't wash.

Lestat the vampire would know, even if his creator has somehow forgotten, that if all the world's suffering really is the work of a Creator, framed by some sort of moral order, then that Creator has botched the job so horribly as to merit the fiercest condemnation. Anyone who has properly understood the message of modern vampire fiction and the entire tradition of literary Satanism will believe, as I firmly believe, that having heard all that Memnoch has to say to him, the Vampire Lestat would spit in his eye and refuse pointblank to have any truck with his dubiously-sanitized Hell. He would tell Memnoch that the Heaven he has seen—which consists of legions of angels glorifying God with transcendentally lovely music—is a place where no sane human being could possibly desire to end up, and that even a human being who did want to go there would be forced to refuse on moral grounds, given Memnoch's explanation of the price of admission. Then, if afforded the chance, Lestat would spit in God's eye too, and tell Him to stuff His reinvented Heaven up His Divine Arse, where it belongs.

What Lestat actually does in the final phase of the story is unworthy of him, and it constitutes a terrible betrayal of the hopeful expectations built up in millions of loyal readers by the previous volumes in the series.

VII.

FIELD OF BROKEN DREAMS

MICHAEL BISHOP'S *BRITTLE INNINGS*

The essence of creativity, according to Arthur Koestler's classic analysis of The Act of Creation, is bisociation: the bringing together of disparate notions in such a way that a kind of cross-fertilization occurs and the compound becomes greater than the mere sum of its parts. Some of the partners brought together in this fashion seem to be made for one another from the very beginning, whereas others initially strike the onlooker as so bizarre as to be virtually unthinkable, but even the most unlikely juxtapositions are capable of synergistic association in the right circumstances.

Brittle Innings is a novel about Frankenstein's monster playing minor league baseball in the American Deep South during World War II. At first sight this may appear to be one of the most ridiculous combinations of motifs ever devised, but Michael Bishop demonstrates that it is not—and, indeed, that there is a unique propriety in it. The fundamental tale which is told in the story is so nearly universal that there are very few lengthy works of fiction which do not contain some form or echo of it, but precisely for this reason it is a tale which cannot be renewed and revivified and given claws to catch the heart without being encoded in some peculiarly striking fashion.

It is possible to discern the meaning and significance of Frankenstein's monster as an allegory of the human predicament purely in terms of the text which created him and

73

its imagistic legacy, and it is possible to discern the meaning and significance of baseball as a microcosm of human hopes and desires without reference to any texts at all, so it is not immediately apparent why the two would benefit from fusion. We know, though, that everything stands out more clearly against a contrasting background and this particular juxtaposition is a contrast indeed. The point, of course, is not simply to make things stand out clearly, but if possible to make the resultant clarity so sharp and so insistent as to burn its image on the brain behind the beholding eye. This task requires an artist of great ability, and the more startling the contrast the greater that ability must be. Michael Bishop has already shown himself to be a writer of considerable skill and consistent grace—not to mention awesome versatility—but *Brittle Innings* is the book which reveals exactly how great his ability is.

Brittle Innings contains three narratives nested one within another. The outer frame is narrated by a sports journalist, explaining how and why he had to make a deal with an aging baseball scout, by which the journalist will get to write the book he wants to write—an educative account of the scout's career—if he first writes a book on his subject's behalf, telling the story which he yearns to tell. The main part of the text is this story: a first-person account of the long-gone season which first raised and then put paid to the scout's hope of being a major-league player. Contained within it, however, is yet another first-person narrative: the partial autobiography of the monster Victor Frankenstein made, whose early career was described in a series of letters written by Robert Walton aboard a vessel trapped in the Arctic ice, which eventually came into the hands of Mary Shelley and were published by her as a "novel."

The protagonist of the main narrative, Danny Boles, is a stammering seventeen-year-old high-school student in Tenkiller, Oklahoma, when he is spotted as a potential professional shortstop by the sister of the owner of a team in the Chattahoochee Valley League (whose territory overlaps the border between Georgia and Alabama). It is 1943 and the draft has decimated the pool of available players; part of Danny's attraction is that he seems unlikely to be judged fit for military service. He gladly signs for the Highbridge Hell-benders and sets off to join them, aware of the irony of the fact that his smidgin of Cherokee blood is travelling the in-famous "trail of tears" in reverse. The journey is nightmar-ish; the GIs with whom the train is crammed look upon him with unanimous naked hatred and he is robbed and raped by a sergeant who claims to know his allegedly-despicable fa-ther. This recalls to Danny's mind the horror of an occasion when his father (whom he has not seen in years) struck him across the throat, with the result that he could not talk at all for two years; he is struck dumb again and arrives at his des-tination speechless.

Partly by virtue of his dumbness and partly by virtue of his protruding ears, Danny is nicknamed Dumbo by his new team-mates. Although they are rough-mannered and bad-tempered most of them treat him reasonably kindly most of the time, but the incumbent shortstop whose rival he has been appointed to be, Buck Hoey, is implacably hostile and hateful from the outset. Danny's nightmare is briefly inten-sified when he is allocated a half-share in a room occupied by the grotesque giant Henry "Jumbo" Clerval, but he comes to realize that this is actually a position of privilege (the gi-ant has never before allowed anyone to share with him). Clerval becomes his protector, and in exchange the infalli-bly-discreet Danny becomes the giant's confidant and con-fessor.

As the season progresses Danny gradually wins a repu-tation as a good player, but it is his awkward relationship with a girl—the daughter of the team's lone middle-aged groupie—which eventually allows him to break through his psychological barrier and recover his voice. In the meantime, news of his father's death is given to him by Franklin D. Roosevelt himself, after a game at which the touring presi-dent has made a morale-boosting appearance. The fates of Danny and the monster become increasingly entwined, com-plicated by deceit and mystery in some matters but secured by honest mutual aid in other and more vital ones; in the end they are a team within a team, one for all and all for one.

The point of all this is, of course, that—as their nick-names suggest—Danny and the monster have a great deal in common. In essence, they are embarked upon precisely the same quest, which is summed up by the title of a book which the monster goes to some trouble to obtain: *On Being a Real Person* by Harry Emerson Fosdick. The monster is a prolific consumer of self-help books—and, for that matter, of books of many other kinds, all of which he seems to approach in much the same earnestly inquisitive fashion.

Since deciding not to end his life in the Arctic wilderness after taking his creator's body from Walton's ship, the monster's sole project has been to fit himself for life in human society, in the hope of one day being accepted therein. By the time that Danny meets him he has contrived to ameliorate the unprepossessing color of his skin and to modify his altogether unnatural height (by surgically excising sections from his own leg-bones without the benefit of anaesthetic). He has become a vegetarian and a pacifist, and is now well-educated and well-spoken. Most important of all, he has found in the baseball diamond the one arena of human affairs where his capabilities will more than compensate for his unfortunate appearance. Through baseball, the monster has a chance of becoming an object of admiration among his potential fellows, if only he can make it into the major league. In essence, all of this is simply Danny's problems and Danny's dreams writ large. He too yearns to become a fully-fledged member of the human race, and he too must overcome a whole series of hurdles carelessly erected for him by his father/creator—whose one and only positive contribution to his life chances was to teach him how to play baseball.

The particular significance of baseball in American life—and hence, of course, in the story—is that it provides a kind of Utopian model of how society is supposed to work in an age of individualism. The performance of the individual, arising out of his own talent, skill, determination, and conformity with the rules, is everything—but everything the individual accomplishes contributes to the performance of the team, seamlessly uniting his personal interests with those of a greater whole (which extends, of course, to all the team's supporters). Like getting married and having children, only much more so, being a baseball player offers a ready-made certificate of belonging to human society, and playing in the major leagues is the ultimate badge of honor.

Unfortunately, the model which looks so wonderful and so perfect in the abstract can only be as good in practice as the society which contains it, and the actual baseball team of which Danny and the monster are parts is riven with all the conflicts of the world without. For instance, the black pitcher who is better by far than any of the players—and is the bastard son of its aristocratic owner—is excluded from the all-white league and forced into a menial role, his superiority in the field of play generating envy and bitter resentment instead of admiration. This is merely the most glaringly obvious of the monstrous injustices, hatreds, and ironies which are scrupulously mirrored in the make-up and behavior of the Hellbenders. It is the marvellous detailing and deft extrapolation of this analogy which provides the measure of Michael Bishop's accomplishment in producing this novel.

The power of *Brittle Innings* to move the reader derives from the fact that although Danny and the monster—like everyone else who ever travelled the reversed trail of tears which leads from childhood to adulthood—are desperate to become "real persons" it does not seem that the people around them are making much use of their own opportunities to do likewise. Nor is it obvious that the society they so earnestly desire to join has much use for members of the worthy sort which they are so ambitious to become. In the end, as we know from the very beginning by courtesy of the frame narrative, Danny's chance to go up to the majors is ruined by Buck Hoey's malice; he must settle for a very different role in the world of baseball—and, perforce, in the world per se. Were he alone in the story this would inevitably seem like his own failure, but he is not alone; if the role which the monster plays were not enough to make it abundantly clear that the failure is, in fact, the world's, the journalist is there to pop up when everything is said and done, still so preoccupied with his own project that he cannot see anything more than a tall tale in the allegory he has been asked to pass on.

Brittle Innings appears to have begun life as a novella (the author's notes include an acknowledgment to a screenwriter who produced a movie script based on some such early version) but its five hundred pages are not in the least excessive. There is not a wasted image or phrase in the text, which is extraordinarily rich and eminently readable from beginning to end. It is a very fine book indeed, and I cannot emphasize too heavily the insistence that no potential reader should allow himself or herself to be put off by the seeming freakishness of its premise. It is not the first good sequel to *Frankenstein* to be produced by an American SF writer—it is at least arguable that the whole "steampunk" craze was kick-started by Steven Utley and Howard Waldrop's stirring "Black as the Pit, from Pole to Pole" (1977)—but *Brittle Innings* seems to me to be the best sequel imaginable, at least for the present. If the story were ever to reach the big screen the resultant movie would surely be a travesty, but if the making of such a movie were to persuade more people to read the book that would be ample justification for the endeavor.

VIII.

THE MAGIC OF THE MOVIES

It has long been recognized that the world of the movies is a foreign country; they do things differently there. Some sixty years has passed since Elmer Rice produced his mock-Utopian romance *A Voyage to Purilia* (1930), in which visitors from our world enter the movie-world and have an absurdly comical time learning to cope with the eccentric metaphysics of cuts, close-ups, and fade-outs, and with the silly paradoxes of *cliché* and censorship. A similar interval separates us from Vicente Huidobro's proud boast that his *Mirror of a Mage* (1931) was a pioneering "visual novel" which would daringly take aboard the methods of "the cinematograph" in order to exploit the particular education of experience which had been visited upon audiences by the silver screen. Since then, history has carried us inexorably into an age when the movies are one of the most significant aspects of our common cultural heritage. We have all become expert in decoding their modes of presentation, and can no longer be surprised to find them mirrored in prose.

As those sixty years have passed, our involvement with the movies has become far more complex and far more intimate. In the 1950s the TV set made the entirety of cinema history potentially available to a single generation of viewers, and freed the consumption of movies from the tyranny of cinema scheduling; in the 1980s the rapid proliferation of video-machines brought about a further liberation, exempting the TV set from the straitjacket of broadcasting schedules. We can now watch most of the films which we

79

want to watch at times of our own choosing in the comfort of our own homes.

These changes have brought about a fundamental change in the relationship between consumers and that great reservoir of visual imagery which is cinema history, allowing the mythological heritage of the cinema to be constantly available to everyone in a way which was never possible before. Broadcast TV preserved that heritage in an essentially disordered fashion, repeating old films endlessly but haphazardly, but the video-library has added the extra dimensions of order and choice to the relationship.

The kind of access which the viewers of today have to films is comparable, for the first time, with the kind of access which readers have to books—with the important difference that there are far fewer films in the world than literary texts, and far more people are interested in them. The imagery of the movies refreshes parts of the population which literary imagery never reaches, and familiarity with particular filmic imagery is shared by far more people than ever shared familiarity with literary images. In fact, all the literary characters who have become household names in the twentieth century—Sherlock Holmes, Dracula, Tarzan, James Bond—have acquired. or at least cemented, their celebrity via the movies.

Part and parcel of this change in our relationship with the movies has been a change in our relationship with the materials of fantasy. Because visual spectacle and violent action are the staples of the popular cinema, the repertoire of the film-director has always been heavily dependent on special effects. Even the making of realistic drama involves the clever and carefully-organized use of stunt men whose substitution for actors is expertly concealed by cutting, and it may also involve the use of elaborate models whose destruction will stand in for the destruction of buildings or whole cities. Techniques like these, supplemented by modern techniques of make-up and methods of splicing images together, make it possible for the cinema to present events impossible in the everyday world in an astonishingly convincing manner. The directors of movies have always used every trick at their disposal to present fictional worlds and events as

80

strange as they could contrive; nowadays, they can offer realistic simulations of worlds and events that are very strange indeed.

From the moment of their inception the movies found a vast heritage of literary images available for predation, and they went to the feast with a rapacious appetite. It was inevitable, as Vicente Huidobro recognized in his own quaint fashion, that there would be a counterflow of influence in the other direction, and we are now beginning to see that flow become a flood. The books from which popular films are made become best-sellers all over again, and novelizations of original film-scripts are safe cash-cows for the publishing industry. The entire genre of horror fiction, which had retired into comfortable esotericism in the early part of the century, has enjoyed a spectacular movie-led boom in the last twenty years.

In view of all this, it is hardly surprising that we find among the literary fantasies produced in 1989 a number of works which deal artfully with the subject of our fascination with the movies, and various aspects of the evolving relationship between viewers and cinematic fantasies. Three in particular stand out: *Ancient Images* by Ramsey Campbell; *A Child Across the Sky* by Jonathan Carroll; and *The Night Mayor* by Kim Newman.

* * * * * * *

Of the three novels under consideration, *Ancient Images* is the most conventional. Its heroine is a film-editor whose colleague—an indefatigable researcher with a keen interest in locating and restoring "lost" films—has discovered a print of a 1930s film starring Boris Karloff and Bela Lugosi which had been suppressed after completion, following the sudden violent death of its director. Tracking down a copy has not been easy because everyone involved in the making of the film felt uneasy about it at the time, and the survivors still feel uneasy—with good reason, given that some of them seem not to have been the same since.

The heroine arrives at the private screening arranged by her friend just in time to see him leap off a roof, apparently fleeing a pursuer she cannot see; the film, of course, is gone. The story then follows the heroine's quest to retrace the course of her dead colleague's enquiries, searching for another copy of the elusive film and for an explanation of his curious death. Her own footsteps are dogged, in the meantime, by shadowy figures she can never quite make out—until the climax, when they and everything else become horribly clear.

Ramsey Campbell is a past master of the suspenseful horror story, and he brings all his careful craftsmanship to the unravelling of this fairly predictable plot. His great strength as a writer is his ability to build sinister elements by slowly-amplified degrees into a narrative which is full of realistic detail, extrapolating the artistic method of M. R. James to novel length. He is almost alone in his ability to do this without relying on grand guignol violence, although he is able to do that too, when his themes require it. The greatest difficulty faced by the writer of suspenseful horror stories of the subtler kind is to maintain the reader's patience and sympathy with a character who cannot know (as the reader inevitably does) that the pattern of events through which the plot moves really are significant of something unutterably nasty, and that it would be more sensible to stop rationalising away their foreboding hints of horror to come; Campbell can do this, and do it well, even in a 299-page novel like *Ancient Images*.

From one viewpoint, *Ancient Images* is simply one more performance of a kind which Campbell has perfected—and in that respect it is not quite up to the very high standard which he set with *The Nameless* (1981) and *Incarnate* (1983), and maintains with his more recent *Midnight Sun* (1990)—but its use of a film as the focal point of the unwinding curse forces it to touch on certain issues which, although not really relevant to the unfolding of the plot, are of interest in themselves.

There is a scene in an early chapter of *Ancient Images* which seems, on the face of it, merely to be a satirical red herring. The heroine, having only just begun her search, visits a group of horror buffs associated with a fanzine, significantly entitled Gorehound, who had been in communication with her dead colleague. It turns out that they cannot help her, and the description of their sick and salivating fascination with the bloodiest scenes of a particularly crude video nasty which they happen to be watching is way over the top by comparison with Campbell's customary deftness—and yet the heroine finds the encounter curiously terrifying. In the fullness of time—although Campbell does not labor the point by any explicit statement—it transpires that this scene does have a certain metaphorical relevance after all, because the ancient images which give the story its title are of a very similar nature to those which flit across the video screen in this brief interlude. The peculiar avidity of the three weird horrorschlock-addicts is exactly what is made incarnate in the supernatural pursuers whose image has been unwisely incorporated in the lost film.

When they are not busy harrying those who have come into contact with their cinematic representation, the monsters in *Ancient Images* have a ritual function to perform, which is aided by the passive acceptance of the morally-anaesthetized inhabitants of the fertile land that they nourish with violently-spilled blood. This carries implications for our judgment of all unthinking "consumers" of horror, wherever they are to be found.

It may seem odd that Campbell, who makes a living writing horror stories, should cast a jaundiced eye upon the motives and appetites of fans of gruesome excess, but one of the key roles of the horror story is, of course, to confront its users with awkward questions about their own impulses, appetites and secret fantasies. Like the heroine of *Ancient Images*, we find that cinematic imagery such as that contained in the film (which she ultimately manages to see) raises such questions much more provocatively than the written story which is its basis (which she reads, but finds unengaging). The relative unsubtlety of cinematic plotting and its lack of space for intricate philosophical discourse inevitably means, however, that careful and intricate consideration of the import of cinema imagery must be left to prose.

* * * * * * *

A Child Across the Sky, whose plot is in some respects very similar to that of *Ancient Images*, is part of a looseknit series of novels by Jonathan Carroll. It borrows characters from both *Bones of the Moon* (1987) and *Sleeping in Flame* (1988), and although it has no actual internal references to the earlier novels *The Land of Laughs* (1980) and *Voice of Our Shadow* (1983), similarities of theme and method bind all of these works together into a common enterprise which, although one hesitates to describe it as "coherent," is certainly a more-or-less unified whole.

The protagonist of *A Child Across the Sky* is Weber Gregston, an earnest and honest but slightly flaky film director who once fell in love with Cullen James, the protagonist of *Bones of the Moon*, and briefly shared her bizarre dreams of the parallel world Rondua. Like the heroine of Ramsey Campbell's novel he is impelled by the mysterious death of a close friend into a search for a missing bit of film—in this case a single scene unaccountably lost from the last of four horror films written by, directed by, and starring the friend in question, Philip Strayhorn. As in *Ancient Images* the search is complicated by the fact that some of the people involved in shooting the missing scene have died in freak accidents, while the sole remaining witness seems to have undergone a radical personality-transplant. What is more, the hunters are themselves hunted—or at least observed—by baleful supernatural entities.

Like Campbell, Carroll is a master of mundane detail, which he deploys very cleverly to give his narratives an effective gloss of realism and to make the reader sympathetic to his characters. His style is, however, markedly different from Campbell's. He is much more sentimental, sometimes even schmaltzy, but a more striking difference is to be seen in the intrusions of the fantastic into his plots, which are by no means M. R. Jamesian. Carroll's fantastic intrusions rarely lurk half-glimpsed in the background; they tend to be introduced rather flatly and their surreality is frequently quite blatant. They usually seem sinister at first only because they are so bizarre, although their innately menacing qualities tend to be exposed by slow degrees as his plots progress.

Carroll has habitually drawn upon the apparatus of childhood, weirdly distorted and abnormally exaggerated, to populate the fantasies which slowly engulf his protagonists: the creations of a hypothetical writer of children's books in *The Land of Laughs*; giant talking toys in *Bones of the Moon*; the Brothers Grimms' fairy tales in *Sleeping in Flame*. Although the plot of *A Child Across the Sky* revolves around a group of horrific slasher movies about a fictitious incarnation of evil called Bloodstone the contents of the films themselves are described very obliquely; what we are mostly told about in connection with them concerns the various childhood experiences which the writer/director star plundered for inspiration. The supernatural character who provides the key to the plot is ostensibly an angel, but she is also the film-maker's imaginary childhood playmate brought to life. She manifests herself in the mock-innocent guise of a nine-year-old girl, who claims to be paradoxically pregnant with the dead man's cancer-stricken girl-friend.

The narrative of *A Child Across the Sky* is much less taut than those to be found in Carroll's earlier works, and it carries a considerable burden of extraneous material. The plot sometime gives the impression that the author is floundering among its convolutions, not altogether certain about what is relevant and what is not. Despite long passages devoted to enlightening the reader about the links between the characters and those of the two preceding books none of those links is of any real consequence, except to remind us repeatedly of the thesis on which their plots turn. That central tenet of Carrollian philosophy is: if that which we delight in imagining were somehow to become real, its actuality would be nightmarish. When applied to horror films, this would seem to be obvious enough, but Carroll is far too skillful a writer to belabor the merely obvious, and he succeeds in making the point unexpectedly sharp with the aid of a particularly ingenious double-twist ending, which is neater than any of those contrived in his earlier works.

The question which is at stake throughout the plot of *A Child Across the Sky* is what the suicidal film-maker achieved by reprocessing the substance of his own and his friends' childhood nightmares into cinematic horrorschlock.

Did he succeed in making evil so glamorous that his films have become a corrupting force? Did he, tacitly or formally, sell his soul to the devil in return for the gift of showing people the hidden horrors of their own inner nature? And did he, in the fortuitously missing scene, succeed so well in pleading Satan's case that he went beyond the permission which God grants for the devil's work to be done on earth? The plot, incessantly scratching away with questions of this kind, gets far enough under the skin of arguments about the power of cinematic images to show up the pathetic simple-mindedness of common-or-garden arguments about kids imitating screen violence, without actually revealing a more sophisticated mode of discourse which might take its place.

* * * * * * *

Both Campbell and Carroll are well-established writers of fiction, with secure reputations, whose use of imaginary films as motifs has slotted into natural places in the sequences of their works. Their use of such motifs is entirely natural, given that Campbell did long service as a film critic and that Carroll's father was a notable Hollywood script-writer (he has also been involved in film-making himself). It is interesting to compare and contrast their efforts with the work of a writer whose career to date has been much more obviously involved with and fascinated by the cinema, but who has only recently turned to the writing of novels: the film critic and historian Kim Newman.

There is an obvious overlap between Newman's career and Ramsey Campbell's, in that the latter's ability to find fascination in the quest to recover a lost horror film of the thirties draws abundantly upon his long experience as a film reviewer. Like many writers of horror fiction Campbell is a very witty speaker, and he occasionally favors SF conventions with hilarious talks on the follies of ancient horror films whose very ineptness makes them enjoyable. The frequent achievement of belated popularity by extraordinarily bad films, which become classics by virtue of their makeshift special effects and desperate plotting is testimony to the expertise which modern viewers very quickly cultivate in seeing the artifice behind cinematic illusions, and being able to laugh at its occasional idiocies. But there is more to this than the mere comedy of incompetence, and our relationship with old, tarnished illusions is also remarkably sentimental; a fact made clear in Ancient Images, and much more elaborately exploited by Newman's fiction. Since Newman turned to novel-writing he has produced cinematic fiction in amazing profusion, and with a uniquely boisterous zest which will surely make him one of the leading fantasy writers of the 1990s. The fortunes of his works may also provide a curious litmus test of the precise extent to which the contemporary mythologies of popular culture have been formed and focused by cinematic imagery.

The Night Mayor is a thriller set in a future where information technology has advanced to the point where the media can hook in directly to people's nervous systems. The equivalent of today's Hollywood hacks are "Dreamers" who assist experience-synthesizing computers with their plotting and characterization, adding a humanly creative touch to what is basically a mechanical process. When an ingenious supercriminal "escapes" from imprisonment by establishing his own private dreamworld within the information network, the only people with the necessary expertise to hunt him down and destroy his dream—lest it expand to corrupt and conquer the entire information-world—are the said hacks. One of them is promptly conscripted by the powers-that-be, which are here uneuphemistically called the Gunmint.

Alas, the first hunter sent into the dream is all-too-quickly absorbed by it and reduced to the status of an imperilled character; a second agent must therefore be conscripted and sent in to rescue and combine forces with him. In order to carry out their mission successfully the two Dreamers must adapt their strategies and expectations to the "rules" of the Secondary World they are invading—which, as it happens, is compounded out of the imagery of a particular sub-genre of the old-fashioned and obsolete "flattie" films whose influence on their own dubious art-form inevitably remains considerable. The sub-genre in question is American films noirs, and the private universe over which the Night Mayor reigns supreme is essentially a compound of all such films, populated by countless avatars of Humphrey Bogart, Edward G. Robinson, and their numerous contemporaries.

The breezily pyrotechnic action and mock-casual style of *The Night Mayor* combine well to make it a very striking book, extraordinarily vivid and very witty. It does not merely borrow the special artifice of the *film noir* to construct its scenarios, but also conducts a quirky interrogation of the essential appeal of such films, and contrives in its own narrative frame to offer a distorted reflection of their assumptions about the possibility of heroism in an institutionally-corrupt world. As a dream-subversion story it is more extravagantly funny than any of its predecessors, and much more intensively recomplicated; it is not a long book (especially by today's word-processor-inflated standards) but it is crammed full of detail and movement in a way which admirably reflects its homage to the cinema.

Despite the nostalgic element in its celebration of *film noir* stereotypes *The Night Mayor* is essentially a book of the video age. Because he has been a film fan for so many years Newman has spent a significant fraction of his adult life watching films in the cinema and on TV (whether broadcast or videotaped). He reads books too, and might reasonably lay claim to being something of a connoisseur of horror fiction as well as the several film genres in which he is most interested, but the world of his imagination is very elaborately stocked with visual imagery inherited from the cinema. His particular stocks are undoubtedly fuller and more coherently-organized than those which most of us have, but they are no longer so different in kind as they would have been ten years ago.

Newman's other fiction is equally cinematic in style and substance although its borrowings are not always so straightforward or so obvious. Indeed, the relationship between *The Night Mayor* and Newman's other works is very interesting in respect of the overlapping of resources and techniques and the transplantation of material from one medium to another. Some reference is made in the course of *The Night Mayor* to a Dreamer named John Yeovil, and there are similar irrelevant references in certain literary works signed Jack Yeovil to a film-maker named Kim Newman; Newman and Yeovil are, of course, one and the same. "Jack Yeovil" has so far only published two novels and a handful of short stories, all of them set in imagined universes derived from games marketed by Games Workshop, but several others are scheduled for release in the near future; the most interesting of these stories in the present context are those set in the imaginary universe of a board game called Dark Future, whose history has been extravagantly elaborated by Newman and Alex Stewart.

Even Yeovil's heroic fantasies show the very heavy influence of the cinema in both method and action. *Drachenfels* (1989) has a quasi-Medieval setting but it concerns the staging of a grand dramatic event, which allows the plot to inflict a series of ghoulish horror-film set-pieces upon actors who are busy reconstructing a horror-film plot of their own. The novel borrows its structure and pace from that most absurdly unlikely of sources, the Busby Berkeley film *Gold Diggers of 1933*. This methodology has much more obvious and extravagant effects, however, on Newman's pseudonymous Dark Future stories, the first four of which are "Route 666" (in the anthology of the same title edited by David Pringle, 1990), *Demon Download* (1990), *Krokodil Tears* (1990), and *Comeback Tour* (1992). All are part of a series which is ostensibly a sequence of violent horror stories concerning the attempts made by an immortal summoner of demons to facilitate an apocalyptic invasion of an alternative earth as it approaches the year 2000. In fact the series—like *The Night Mayor*—is really a comedy, because its horror motifs and its graphic violence are used to comic effect, in a fashion which is much more familiar in the cinema (and also in comic books) than in text stories.

The cinema's tradition of comic violence is, of course, well-established—it goes back to the visual gags employed in silent films and extends through countless cartoons of the Tom-and-Jerry variety. The tradition of comic horror is of more recent provenance, first becoming obvious in certain films made by Roger Corman and continuing into such modern classics as *The Evil Dead*. In both traditions, though, film-makers exploit the fact that the viewer knows that what is happening is a mere illusion of animation or "special effects" in order to to make chains of events which would seem utterly horrible if they were assumed to be real into macabre jokes. Literary equivalents of the same strategy can be found in many items of urban folklore and in stories by such writers as Robert Bloch.

The relationship between the viewers of comic horror films and their material is essentially that of the connoisseur rather than the consumer, because the normal conventions by which the viewer suspends disbelief and pretends that what is happening on screen is real are teasingly called into question, requiring the simultaneous comprehension of two narrative levels. Newman does exactly the same thing in his Yeovil novels—which must not be read naïvely if they are to be properly appreciated. (Undoubtedly there will be some onlookers who, like the diehard opponents of comic-book horror, will think them quasi-pornographic, but they will be missing the point, as they invariably do.) Some of the jokes are glaringly obvious but effectively trivial—like the parody of Hitchcock's *Psycho* which figures in *Krokodil Tears*—but others are awesome in their temerity. The invocation of the Lone Ranger as *deus ex machina* in *Demon Download* is the kind of thing which writers rarely dare to do when operating under their own names for fear of being thought silly, while the re-costuming of the infamous Tasmanian Devil (familiar to fans of animated cartoons) as an all-too-human psychotic mass-murderer sets new standards in sick flamboyance.

The Jack Yeovil novels belong to a literary subspecies which constitutes the despised undergrowth of contemporary SF and fantasy—the Shared World story. Like B-movies, therefore, they operate on the margins of a field which is already marginal in terms of its cultural respectability; like the best (and worst) B-movies, however, they undoubtedly have the potential to attract a cult following and enjoy subsequent recognition as revealing and fascinating products of their time and their art. The Dark Future novels in particular exhibit a glorious lack of inventive inhibition which Newman might not be able to keep up forever, and they should be treasured while they last. *The Night Mayor* aspires to a higher level of literary sophistication, but it is mercifully content to be a modest kind of Main Feature; Newman may have absorbed the lessons of cinema history sufficiently to approach with caution the idea that his natural destiny is to make big-budget super-epics. His second novel under his own name, *Bad Dreams* (1990) is similarly uninflated, but rather more substantial than *The Night Mayor*; its cinematic borrowings are more subdued, but nevertheless obvious to the alert eye.

Like all pioneers, Kim Newman may face some difficulties in attracting an audience into what is effectively an undercolonized literary niche. The English-language publishing industry is nowadays so obsessive about standardized packaging that it routinely mistreats authors who do not quite fit, and it is not impossible that Newman may suffer the temporary indignity of seeing his work marketed by publishers and booksellers as "horror" to people who will frown at his irreverence for the schlocky icons of their standard fare (nor is it impossible that the entire GW Books project, and "Jack Yeovil" with it, will founder on the rock of its own dilettantism, which has so far been expressed in atrocious book-design, haphazard scheduling and incompetent distribution). He is, however, far too good a writer to be obliterated by such accidents of fate; he deserves to be reckoned the most energetic, vivacious and colorful member of the emergent generation of British fantasy-writers.

* * * * * * *

Kim Newman's wholesale borrowing of cinematic artifice and its peculiar aesthetics is mostly in the cause of fun, but *Bad Dreams* does begin to exploit the horrific aspects of modern cinematic imagery more straightforwardly, and to an effect which is much more scarifying than flip or comic. Like Ramsey Campbell, Newman is aware of the fact that the obsessive fascination which some people have developed for cinematic nastiness is itself rather scary, and cause for anxiety. A film critic, who must maintain a certain distance from the objects of his appraisal, in perhaps not the best person to tackle this anxiety head on, but the relevance of Newman's work is not significantly compromised by its calculated irreverence. Carroll's examination of the issue is more dignified and more earnest, as one would expect from a former teacher of courses in world literature, but it is curiously subverted by his own apparent doubts about the true lesson to be learned from Philip Strayhorn's remarkable career.

In the end, the particular magic of Boris Karloff, Bela Lugosi, and Bloodstone is as elusive as the bits of film containing that magic which the central characters of *Ancient Images* and *A Child Across the Sky* chase hither and yon, without ever quite catching up with them. Similarly, the shadowy black-and-white world where it always seems to be raining can never be stabilized even in the powerful fixative imagination of the *Night Mayor* and or his gone-native pursuer. Such images have already burrowed so deeply into the fantastic inner world of our private thoughts and daydreams that they have become as ominously mysterious to us as our own dreams.

The imagery of the movies is now part of the hard core of our shared experiences of fantasy, which allows us to communicate with one another through the media of jokes and allusions, scary tales and convoluted allegories. Because that imagery is so vivid it helps enliven our lives; and because it is shared it does its bit to help bind us together into a community of like-minded beings; but because it has its nightmarish aspects, it also feeds our common anxieties. All of this is amply displayed in *Ancient Images*, *A Child Across the Sky*, and *The Night Mayor*, and we are likely to encounter much more of it in the fantastic fiction of the 1990s.

* * * * * * *

Say, who was that masked man, anyhow—and what was that thing that I couldn't quite make out...???

* * * * * * *

NOTE (1995): The entire GW Books project did indeed founder on the rock of its own dilettantism, and seems to have foundered yet again after a temporary resurrection by Boxtree—but "Jack Yeovil" continues to produce books for other publishers and seems likely to continue his shadow career for some time to come.

SLAVES OF THE DEATH SPIDERS, BY BRIAN STABLEFORD

IX.

H. G. WELLS AND THE DISCOVERY OF THE FUTURE

On 24 January 1902 H. G. Wells delivered a lecture to the Royal Institution, whose text was subsequently published under the title, "The Discovery of the Future." The lecture was, in effect, a series of afterthoughts to his pioneering work of futurology, *Anticipations of the Reaction of Mechanical and Human Progress upon Human Life and Thought* (1901), which was by then entering its fifth edition. Wells began the lecture by describing two types of mind, whose outlook on life is sharply contrasted:

> It will lead into my subject most conveniently to contrast and separate two divergent types of mind, types which are to be distinguished chiefly by their attitude towards time, and more particularly by the relative importance they attach and the relative amount of thought they give to the future of things.
> The first of these two types of mind—and it is, I think, the predominant type, the type of the majority of living people—is that which seems scarcely to think of the future at all, which regards it as a sort of black non-existence upon which the advancing present will presently write events. The second type, which is, I think, a more modern and much

less abundant type of mind, thinks constantly, and by preference, of things to come, and of present things mainly in relation to the results that must arise from them. The former type of mind, when one gets it in its purity, is retrospective in habit, and it interprets the things of the present, and gives value to this and denies it to that, entirely with relation to the past. The latter type of mind is constructive in habit; it interprets the things of the present and gives value to this or that, entirely in relation to things designed or foreseen.

While from that former point of view our life is simply to reap the consequences of the past, from this our life is to prepare the future. The former type one might speak of as the legal or submissive type of mind, because the business, the practice, and the training of a lawyer dispose him towards it; he of all men must most constantly refer to the law made, the right established, the precedent set, and most consistently ignore or condemn the thing that is only seeking to establish itself. The latter type of mind I might for contrast call the legislative, creative, organising, or masterful type, because it is perpetually falling away from respect for what the past has given us. It sees the world as one great workshop, and the present as no more than material for the future, for the thing that is yet destined to be. It is in the active mood of thought, while the former is in the passive; it is the mind of youth—it is the mind most manifest among the Western nations; while the former is the mind of age—the mind of the Oriental.

Things have been, says the legal mind, and so we are here. And the creative mind says, We are here, because things have yet to be.[1]

Wells goes on in his talk, as one might expect, to champion the second kind of thinking—the kind of thinking which is future-orientated. He concedes that this kind of mental orientation is more difficult to support than the other, pointing out that we have certain knowledge of the past, thanks to memory and history, but none of the future. He goes on to suggest, however, that although we can have no insight into the future which resembles memory, we might be able to provide something which could bear analogy with history. He backs up this suggestion with the argument that much of what we know of the past comes not from recorded memories but from inferences drawn from discovered data— he refers, of course, to the revelations of what were in his time emerging sciences: geology, archeology and palaeontology. Given that our knowledge of the past is inferential, he says, can we not hope to infer some knowledge of the future from relevant data?

Wells had already begun, in *Anticipations*, to practise what he preached in this lecture, and all his subsequent futuristic speculations—including those cast as fiction—were constrained by his futurological ambitions. He devoted himself ever more intently to the business of attempting to predict the actual course of events which would emerge from the confusion of possibility.

* * * * * * *

Anticipations and "The Discovery of the Future" marked a crucial change of direction in the character of Wells's thought and work. The lecture was delivered shortly after the publication of the last of his classic scientific romances, *The First Men in the Moon*—which had been preceded by *The Time Machine, The Island of Dr. Moreau, The Invisible Man, The War of the Worlds, When the Sleeper Wakes*, and three collections of short stories, all issued between 1895 and 1901. "The Discovery of the Future" can be seen in retrospect as the crucial punctuation mark which put a stop to that phase of his career, which had celebrated a rather different "discovery of the future."

SLAVES OF THE DEATH SPIDERS, BY BRIAN STABLEFORD

A century has now passed since the first book publication of H. G. Wells's *The Time Machine*. A similar span of
time separated the young Wells (who was then in his late
twenties) from the era in which the Comte du Buffon and
Georges Cuvier had first proved, beyond all reasonable
doubt, that the history of the Earth had to be reckoned in
hundreds of millions of years rather than in mere thousands,
and that the human species was a very recent arrival on the
prehistoric scene. Many people realized that those discoveries about the past ought to make us think differently about
the future but Wells was one of the first writers to begin the
work of exploring the possible futures which could now be
glimpsed in the mind's eye. In order to pursue this quest he
came up with the ingenious idea of equipping the hero of his
story with a machine to transport him through time.

The speculations about man's future which formed the
basis of *The Time Machine* were first set out in 1888 in a series of essays called "The Chronic Argonauts" in the students' magazine of the Royal College of Science, *The Science Schools Journal*, which Wells had founded. There was
also a intermediate version serialized as "The Time Traveller's Story" in *The National Observer* in 1894 before a version closer to the book text appeared as a serial in *The New
Review* between January and May 1895. The book itself followed immediately thereafter.

Between the first and second published versions of *The
Time Machine* Wells had been pursuing his literary ambitions by publishing brief essays on scientific matters in various periodicals, most importantly *The Pall Mall Gazette* and
The Saturday Review. The popular magazines of the day
were engaged in fierce competition for market space and
were avid to try out any material that might catch the public
fancy; Wells cultivated both novelty and extravagance in a
series of speculative flights of fancy which extrapolated
items of scientific possibility or mildly controversial propo-
sitions to some gaudy extreme.

Among Wells' essays of this period were "The Dream
Bureau" (*PMG* 25 Oct. 1893), "The Man of the Year Mil-
lion" (*PMG* 6 Nov. 1893), "Angels, Plain and Coloured"
(*PMG* 6 Dec. 1893); later endeavors in the same vein in-

cluded "The Limits of Individual Plasticity" (*SR* 19 Jan. 1895) and "Intelligence on Mars" (*SR* 4 Apr. 1896). Following the spectacular success of *The Time Machine* Wells began systematically to use the ideas explored in such essays as the bases for plots. Although he never wrote a story about dream-addicts ordering a night's entertainment from a catalogue, or the man of the year million lying helplessly in his nutrient tank, the essay on angels provided him with the central motif of *The Wonderful Visit* (1895), in which an angel from the Land of Dreams is shot down by a sporting vicar. The essay on "plasticity" was the basis for *The Island of Dr. Moreau* (1896), in which the eponymous surgeon remakes animals in the image of man and tries (unsuccessfully, in the end) to provide them with the essentials of moral law and the. The essay about intelligent life on Mars was the seed of *The War of the Worlds* (1898), in which the inhabitants of a resource-depleted Mars decide that they will claim the treasures of the earth.

Within three years Wells had developed a method of procedure that laid the foundations of a whole new genre of fiction. The reviewers of the day labelled it "scientific romance"—a label which Wells initially adopted, then discarded, but finally accepted when Gollancz issued an omnibus edition of his most notable speculative novels as *The Scientific Romances of H. G. Wells* in 1933. By that time, however, a new label had been imported from America, and the sheer weight of the material which flooded the British market after World War II ensured that the American label—"science fiction"—would eventually become definitive.

There had, of course, been many tales of the future published before 1895. Many future Utopias had appeared, and the fledgling genre of future war stories had enjoyed a considerable vogue in Britain since George Chesney's remarkable essay in alarmism, *The Battle of Dorking*, had appeared in *Blackwood's Magazine* in 1871. What Wells initially did, however, was markedly different from what anyone had done before. He set up the whole spectrum of rapidly-advancing scientific discovery as a generator of possibilities, each one of which might contain the germ of a story. The Utopian writers were interested in designing the ideal society and the writers of future war stories were interested in describing the next war, but Wells produced a way of working which tacitly accepted that the future was an infinite array of competing and conflicting possibilities. From this cloud of potential the course of history would be precipitated by the complex interaction of circumstance, chance and choice.

Wells never devoted himself exclusively to this method of working. He had other ambitions, and he knew that he would not be taken seriously by literary critics unless he wrote "real" novels like *Love and Mr Lewisham* (1900). For a brief period, though, he made spectacular progress within the genre he had pioneered. As well as the novels mentioned above he produced three more full-length scientific romances and a host of shorter works. *The Invisible Man* (1897) is a fine thriller which has frequently been adapted for the stage, the cinema, and TV, cleverly exploiting the special effects of all three media. *When the Sleeper Wakes* (1899) is a story of future revolution precipitated by the revival of a man placed in suspended animation in our own day. *The First Men in the Moon* (1901) is a classic tale of two unlikely friends who employ an anti-gravity device to transport a space-capsule to the moon. The best of his early short stories were collected in three volumes: *The Stolen Bacillus and Other Incidents* (1895), *The Plattner Story and Others* (1897), and *Tales of Space and Time* (1899), the last consisting entirely of scientific romances.

After 1895 Wells never ventured quite as far into the future as he had in *The Time Machine*. The Time Traveller promises at the end of the book that he will come back and tell the people who have listened to his story about his further adventures, but Wells never used his fictitious machine again. He seems, in fact, to have begun to move almost immediately towards the conclusion that he reached and clarified in "The Discovery of the Future": that he had found a better method of exploring the future—one which could not see nearly as far, but which had the compensating advantage of greater accuracy. It was this new method which he set out, and tried to justify, in his lecture.

* * * * * * *

100

Although Wells continued to write futuristic fiction after composing his lecture for the Royal Institution, it was never quite the same in its nature. *The Food of the Gods and How It Came to Earth*, published in 1904, begins as a robust scientific romance, but is soon diverted into another channel, and concludes with the creation of a race of human giants who are a crystallization of Wells's notion of the future-orientated mind: the exponents of a new wisdom and a new spiritual strength. Virtually all Wells's subsequent speculative fiction was to focus in like fashion on the contrasts between the men of his own world and hypothetical New Men who would—or, at least, should—ultimately replace them and become the custodians of progress.

Wells was to go on to write several more Utopian novels, including *A Modern Utopia* (1905), *Men Like Gods* (1923), and the quasi-documentary, *The Shape of Things to Come* (1933), which formed the basis of the famous film *Things to Come* (1935). He also began writing future war stories, anticipating the advent of the tank in "The Land Ironclads" (1903), revising his early scepticism about the usefulness of aircraft in war in *The War in the Air* (1908), and designing a peculiar kind of atom bomb in *The World Set Free* (1914). (He also prepared a revised version of *When the Sleeper Wakes* in 1910 called *The Sleeper Awakes* to take aboard his second thoughts about aerial warfare.)

As a predictor of things to come Wells scored more successes than any of his contemporaries, and his record remains second to none, but the simple fact is that no predictor is or ever will be capable of calculating the actual course of future events. The confluence of circumstance, chance and choice is far too complicated, and contains far too many unknowns, to be reduced to mere calculation. By injecting futurological concentration and Utopian scheming into his futuristic fiction Wells hoped to make it more serious, but all he succeeded in doing was filling it with failed guesses—some of which would, in time, come to seem silly.

Wells was to coin many names for the hypothetical "new men" who would conclusively set aside the follies of he present. They were New Republicans, Samurai, or Men

Like Gods; they were members of a Open Conspiracy or servants of an Air Dictatorship. In his more modest representations they are enlightened contemporaries, intellectuals who have heeded the Wellsian message; in his more fantastic parables they are men miraculously transformed, perhaps by the gases of a marvellous comet or cosmic rays beamed at Earth by Martians—but either way, the future is theirs. His most elaborate futuristic fantasy of the period between the two world wars, *The Shape of Things to Come* ends with the following statement:

> By means of education and social discipline the normal human individual today acquires characteristics without which his continued existence would be impossible. In the future, as the obscurer processes of selection are accelerated and directed by eugenic effort, these acquired characteristics will be incorporated with his inherent nature, and his educational energy will be released for further adaptations. He will become generation by generation a new species, differing more widely from that weedy, tragic, pathetic, cruel, fantastic, absurd and sometimes sheerly horrible being who christened himself in a mood of oafish arrogance Homo sapiens.[2]

Once Wells was well into this second phase of his career as a futurist he developed a certain distaste for the products of his earlier phase. He began to make unkind comments about his own early scientific romances, and his introduction to an omnibus issued under the title *Scientific Romances* in 1933 is remarkably condescending toward them, suggesting that they were exercises in youthful exuberance, not to be taken too seriously. The majority of readers have never agreed, and those early works are still read very frequently, while hardly anyone would bother to look at *A Modern Utopia* or *Men Like Gods*, let alone *The Work, Wealth and Happiness of Mankind* or *The Open Conspiracy*.

* * * * * * *

The difference between Wells's two discoveries of the future can be seen in an observation made by the French writer Anatole France, in his excellent philosophical novel *The White Stone* (1905). This novel, like Wells's lecture, is basically a discussion of whether, how and to what extent we can anticipate the future, and its conclusions are much more pessimistic than Wells's.

When men try to conjure up visions of the future, France suggests, they can usually do no more than project their own hopes or fears into its hypothetical space, building from them images of Utopia or nightmare which, though they pretend to be futuristic, are all too firmly anchored in the present. Thus, France's own vision of a Marxian Communist state of the future is ironically and modestly juxtaposed with a story in which Roman intellectuals in exile, who encounter St. Paul on his travels, see no future in this Christian craziness, but look forward instead to a regeneration of the glory of the empire under its cultured and charismatic new emperor: Nero. In coming to this pessimistic conclusion, however, France notes one remarkable exception to his rule about futuristic visions: the early H. G. Wells, who is nominated by France as the only man ever to have journeyed imaginatively into the future without deciding in advance what he would find. Unfortunately, by the time France published this compliment it had ceased to be true. By 1905 Wells had rediscovered the future, and he was bent on revealing it rather than exploring it.

Wells's second discovery was, of course, an unwitting and unfortunate reversion to an earlier way of thinking. Men have always been interested in the future, and throughout history there have been individuals who were prepared to organize their actions entirely in respect of possible future rewards. All the literate societies which have passed on their ideas to us had their images of the future: images of the temporal future, which were Utopian in kind, and images of the spiritual future, which were eschatological in kind. Different societies in different eras varied quite markedly in the degree of their optimism or pessimism in respect of these different images, but pessimism in respect of the first has always been compensated by an increase of faith in the second. Where belief in worldly progress waned, faith in the possibility of a future life beyond this one waxed. Almost throughout the recorded history of the Western world, men have believed that the future could be known, and their own fate determined by inference from the relevant data.

Wells was born at an important time in the history of ideas. The traditional faith which provided the data from which knowledge of the future could supposedly be inferred was in a state of terminal decay. The validity of the account of the nature of the world contained in the Bible had been devastated by discoveries in those sciences which Wells cited as the sources of our true knowledge of the past. Geology, archeology, and palaeontology pointed to an account of the world very different from the one contained in the Book of Genesis, and Charles Darwin had published an account of the origin and nature of man which decisively challenged traditional ideas of the relationship between men and God. It is significant that the force of these new ideas came to Wells himself with the shattering impact of a sudden enlightenment, when he attended lectures by Thomas Henry Huxley at what was then the London School of Normal Science in he late 1880s. This severance of the relationship between man and God was of fundamental importance with respect to the ideas about the future possessed by ordinary men and women. If religious faith had been mistaken in its account of human creation and human nature, then it might also be wrong in its account of human destiny. The future, which had been known in terms of Heaven and Hell and the return of Christ to Earth to institute his Millennarian reign, was now unknown again. The ancient discovery was abolished, and in its place there was a void.

The inevitable result of this devastation of the eschatological image of the future was a renewal of interest in the temporal image of the future. There grew up in Europe several kinds of futuristic fiction, which claimed attention precisely because of this new uncertainty. Movements calling for various kinds of political reform began to produce images of the future reflecting their ambitions and their anxieties. Their ambitions were reflected primarily in Utopian fantasies of society improved by technological innovations and democratic reorganization. Their anxieties were reflected in fantasies of future war and natural catastrophes. By the 1890s, when Wells began to write prolifically, these subspecies of speculative fiction were merging into the new genre of scientific romance, which was for a while taken up and promoted by the editors of the new middlebrow periodicals that flourished in the period. The origins of the genre in this particular kind of crisis is evident in the fact that many of the early contributors to the genre were the sons of clergymen who were converted to freethought: examples include George Griffith, M. P. Shiel, William Hope Hodgson, J. D. Beresford, C. J. Cutcliffe Hyne, and Grant Allen.

The future that these writers discovered was a future that had not the protective armor of destiny. It was a future that could not be contained within any particular vision, but which could only be exemplified by the sum of them all: it was a future in which there were many possible worlds, desirable and undesirable, probably much altered and possibly quite bizarre. The significance of Wells as a trend-setter and major inspiration to other scientific romancers lies in the spectacular open-mindedness of his early fiction. He used the future not simply as an arena into which he could extrapolate his prejudices, but as a space in which he could carry out bold thought-experiments, testing hypotheses by extravagant display. No one else was ever as good at seizing upon tiny windows of possibility opened by scientific theory or technological expertise and projecting through them powerful searchlights to explore their possible implications, unhindered by the choking constrictions of belief. Wells became the great pioneer of hypothetical fiction, which began the vital work of making clear what a vast range of alternative possibilities the future might hold. He and those who joined him in the writing of scientific romance were the men who realized how extraordinary the future might be; how dramatically the life of men might be transfigured, in many possible ways, by new discoveries in science or by interaction with strange things that might already exist—the product of their own processes of evolution—in other parts of the universe.

The change that overtook Wells in 1902, however, reflected a change that could be seen in the genre as a whole. Anxiety about the future took a much firmer hold in Britain than hope for the future. This is not to say that scientific romance became entirely pessimistic, and certainly not to suggest that futurological speculation ceased to be constructive, but where optimism survived it was a defensive kind of optimism, fully aware of a series of threats which loomed over contemporary men and threatened to overwhelm them before they could discover any temporal salvation to replace the abandoned Christian paradise. Certainly, the two major writers of scientific romance who came to prominence after 1902 but before 1914—Hodgson and Beresford—were conspicuously more pessimistic in their fiction than Griffith, Wells, or Shiel. Even Shiel, whose major works were published after the turn of the century, exhibited a rather peculiar species of defiant optimism which exhorted passionate faith in progress no matter what horrors the future might bring; the moral of his most famous work, *The Purple Cloud* (1901), is that one must believe in the positive thrust of progress even if civilization is obliterated and almost the entire population of the world annihilated. The best of the scientific romances which Wells wrote after 1902, *The War in the Air*, is a novel which parades an anxiety about the destruction of civilization in uncompromising form, and in other similar fictions—including *The World Set Free* and *The Shape of Things to Come*—Wells readily accepts such appalling destruction as part of the price of progress.

The force of this anxiety is easy enough to detect in stories of natural catastrophe and future war. The smallness and insignificance of the world of man had been made clear by sciences which had revealed the true size of the universe and the true antiquity of the earth. Now that the God of the Old Testament was no longer credited with responsibility for visiting floods and plagues upon His people, He could no longer be credited with responsibility for protecting them either. The march of science was seen to be giving men command of ever greater forces, but there were many reasons for supposing that men would rather use those forces to destroy than to create.

The Great War, when it came in 1914, reinforced these anxieties very powerfully. It obliterated one species of optimism that had flourished beforehand: the idea that if men were to fight a new and horribly destructive war, then it would be the final war—the war that would end war. This was the kind of slogan under which the Great War was marketed to those who were recruited in hundreds of thousands to fight in it and die in it, but it quickly came to be seen as a sick joke. The lesson of the Great War, as far as the kind of British mind that was orientated to the future rather than the past was concerned, was that civilization was very fragile, and that contemporary men were living on the lip of an abyss, into which their whole world might easily be plunged by the recklessness of fools. Those future-orientated men who took as their mission the mapping of an historical course by which men might be navigated to a safer world knew well enough how hazardous that course might be, and how desperate their task had become—but they found it hard to find an audience. Scientific romance waned in popularity after the war, and it seemed that many people had taken a different lesson from the horrors of the war—the lesson that the kind of thinking which brooded too much on the future was too difficult and uncomfortable to be borne.

* * * * * * *

Even before the war H. G. Wells had been prepared to imagine himself a sighted man in a country of the blind, unable to convince his contemporaries of the narrowness of their sensations. Afterwards, he found his efforts to awaken others from their willful lack of foresight so difficult that the characterized the new era as the Age of Frustration (a title which he applies to it in *The Shape of Things to Come* and explores more fully in a most peculiar book called *The Anatomy of Frustration*). Other writers of scientific romance echoed this notion, and Wellsian Frustration is acutely obvious in the writings of men who began to produce scientific romances in the period between the wars, including Neil Bell, S. Fowler Wright, John Gloag, and Olaf Stapledon.

The literary response to this Age of Frustration was mixed, but predominant among its moods were a fierce, cynical irony and an angry pessimism. The future war stories published between the wars present a whole series of images of mankind bombed back to the stone age, which develop a terrible fascination as they revel in the details of mass destruction.

At one extreme the scientific romance of the period between the wars was fatalistic almost to the point of nihilism. In the words of Neil Bell:

> And when he was nineteen the War of 1914-18 came, and he went through that long infamy, and came out with no shred or tatter of his former illusions to cover his nakedness.
>
> "Everything failed the common man in that testing," he said. "The church of God, that should have held itself aloof and denounced the rottenness of it all, failed to make that gesture, and setting itself rather to fan the flames, sealed its own fate in the hearts of the men who fought. We saw incompetence that slaughtered thousands shielded by the privilege of birth or wealth or political pull; we saw lying, treachery and greed enthroned and triumphant; we saw lust and cruelty shrieking from safe places the hatred that was unknown to the men who stumbled blindly in the bloody quagmires of mud and pain and hopelessness...
>
> "And so we emerged from that struggle believing in nothing, hardly in ourselves."[3]

And in the words of S. Fowler Wright:

> We are looking at a civilisation without control, and without the freedom that control gives. We are a nation of slaves, and slaves to

a tyrant that we cannot kill, being beyond our
reach. Our new rulers are the aggregate folly
and the aggregate weakness of mankind.
Comfort and cowardice are the new gods.[4]

Where writers sought for hope—as they all did, in their
various ways—they sometimes found it in the idea of a cy-
clical history, whereby civilization would destroy itself utterly over and over again only to be rebuilt anew, much as
every dark night is followed by a new dawn. If this cycle
were to be broken, though, the writers of scientific romance
could imagine that break only in terms of some radical transformation of human nature—the replacement of Homo
sapiens by a new and finer species. This image recurs in the
work of all the major and several of the minor writers of the
period, most obviously in the work of Stapledon, who
chronicled the history of a whole series of human species in
Last and First Men. The most misanthropic writers of the
period could hardly wait for their contemporaries to be hustled off the stage of history and replaced, and the most extreme works of this kind reached a fine pitch of hysteria. The
following is from *This Was Ivor Trent* by Claude Houghton:

And then I turned and saw—You! Your
figure was shrouded, but your face was fully
revealed. It was the countenance of a new
order of Being. I knew that a man from the
future stood before me.
Terror overwhelmed me—then. But I do
not fear you—now.
I stretch out my arms and invoke you:
Come!
I do not know whether you stand on the
threshold, or whether unnumbered ages
separate us from you. I only know that you
must be: that you are the spiritual
consciousness made flesh: that you are the
risen man and that we are the dead men. Yet,
in us, is the possibility of you.

We are the Old—the dying—Consciousness. You are the New—the living—
Consciousness. We have violated earth. You
will redeem it. We descend the darkening
valley of knowledge. You stand on the
uplands of wisdom. We are an end. You are a
beginning.

If you are a dream, all else is a
nightmare. But I have seen God's signature
across your forehead.

Come!

More and more fiercely we deny our
need of you. We say you are a fantasy, a lie,
an illusion. We madden ourselves with
sensation; drug ourselves with work, pleasure,
speed; herd in the vast sepulchres of our
cities; blind our eyes; deaden our ears; cling
to our creed of comfort (Comfort! the last of
the creeds!); sink day by day in deeper and
deeper servitude to our inventions--hoping to
numb the knowledge of our emptiness;
striving to ease the ache of separation; trying
to evade your challenge; seeking to deny our
destiny.

Come!

The martyred earth waits for you. Daily,
our darkness deepens. Secretly, all are afraid.
None knows what to do. To underpin, to
patch up, to whitewash sepulchres—these are
the substitutes for action. To shout, to boast,
to nickname bankruptcy. Prosperity—this is
the substitute for leadership. We have
glorified ourselves, magnified ourselves,
made gods of ourselves. We have served
Hate, Greed, Lust. and now darkness deepens
around us. And we are afraid.

Come!

Lacking you, there is no solution to any
one of our problems. Possessing you, no
problems exist. If it be madness to believe in

you, the sanity which denies you is a greater madness.

But we who have lived on substitutes; we who have plumbed the abyss of ourselves; we who have glimpsed the magnitude of man's misery—we do not deny you.

From the midnight of madness we stretch out our arms to you.

Come![5]

As the thirties progressed it became increasingly obvious to the future-orientated mind that the new war was imminent, and that some kind of radical change in human affairs was easily imaginable. A kind of summary of the ambitions and achievements of scientific romance was provided by Olaf Stapledon in *Star Maker* (1937), in which a man walking alone on a hillside after quarrelling with his wife attempts through a series of visions to place his predicament in its true context, bracketing it within the real dimensions of space, time, and metaphysics, and returning finally to the lonely hillside, where he must decide how he, as an individual, is to orientate himself in respect of a terribly threatening future:

It seemed that in the coming storm all the dearest things must be destroyed. All private happiness, all loving, all creative work in art, science and philosophy, all intellectual scrutiny and speculative imagination, and all creative social building; all, indeed, that should normally live for, seemed folly and mockery and mere self-indulgence in the presence of public calamity. But if we failed to preserve them, when would they live again?

How to face such an age? How to muster courage, being capable only of homely virtues? How to do this, yet preserve the mind's integrity, never to let the struggle destroy in one's own heart what one tried to serve in the world, the spirit's integrity?

Two lights for guidance. The first, our little glowing atom of community, with all that it signifies. The second, the cold light of the stars, symbol of the hypercosmical reality, with its crystal ecstasy.[6]

* * * * * * *

World War II, when it actually arrived, proved a little less terrible than the writers of scientific romance had feared. Poison gas was not used, and the tactics of *Blitzkrieg* failed to destroy civilization. In the manner of its ending, though, the war disqualified the optimism which might otherwise have been fostered by its failure to obliterate civilization. The advent of the atom bomb seemed to confirm all the long-standing fears about man's capacity for world destruction, and revelations of the crimes committed in Germany's concentration camps and death-camps did nothing to assuage fears about the vulnerability of *Homo sapiens* to the corruptions of brutality.

The inevitable reaction to the lesson of World War II was a brief intensification of cynicism and pessimism—a combination best exemplified by what might be considered the last of the great scientific romances, George Orwell's *Nineteen Eighty-Four* (1949). Wells, nearing the end of his life, did not need to wait for Hiroshima to come to his own conclusions about the implications of the new war. In 1945 he published his final book, *Mind at the End of Its Tether*, which he introduced with the following paragraph:

This little book brings to a conclusive end the series of essays, memoranda, pamphlets, through which the writer has experimented, challenged discussion, and assembled material bearing upon the fundamental nature of life and time. So far as fundamentals go, he has nothing more and never will have anything more to say.[7]

He went on to make the following deliberately casual claims:

> Our universe is not merely bankrupt; there remains no dividend at all; it has not simply liquidated; it is going clean out of existence, leaving not a wrack behind. The attempt to trace a pattern of any sort is absolutely futile.
>
> This is acceptable to the philosophical mind when it is at its most philosophical, but for those who lack that steadying mental backbone, the vistas such ideas open are so uncongenial and so alarming, that they can do nothing but hate, repudiate, scoff at and persecute those who express them, and betake themselves to the comfort and control of such refuges of faith and reassurance as the subservient fear-haunted mind has contrived for itself and others throughout the ages.
>
> Our doomed formicary is helpless as the implacable Antagonist kicks or tramples our world to pieces. Endure it or evade it; the end will be the same, but the evasion systems involve unhelpfulness at the least and in most cases blind obedience to egotistical leaders, fanatical persecutions, panics, hysterical violence and cruelty.
>
> After all the present writer has no compelling argument to convince the reader that he should not be cruel or mean or cowardly. Such things are also in his own make-up in a large measure, but none the less he hates and fights against them with all his strength. He would rather our species ended its story in dignity, kindliness and generosity, and not like drunken cowards in a daze or poisoned rats in a sack. But this is a matter of

individual predilection for everyone to decide
for himself.

A series of events has forced upon the
intelligent observer the realisation that the
human story has already come to an end and
that Homo sapiens, as he has been pleased to
call himself, is in his present form played out.
The stars in their courses have turned against
him and he has to give place to some other
better animal better adapted to face the fate
that closes in more and more swiftly upon
mankind.

That new animal may be an entirely alien
strain, or it may arise as a new modification
of the hominidae, and even as a direct
continuation of the human phylum, but it will
certainly not be human. There is no way out
for Man but steeply up or steeply down.
Adapt or perish, now as ever, is Nature's inexorable imperative.[8]

In this fashion, the future discovered by Wells and his
contemporaries reached virtual closure, recapitulating by
analogy the journey made by the Time Traveller in *The Time
Machine*—who witnessed the death of the human species,
and of the earth itself, at the end of an historical sequence
which the younger Wells had regarded only as a flight of serious fancy.

* * * * * * *

Wells's earlier discovery of the future did not, however,
go to waste. He may have forsaken it in favor of another, far
narrower, discovery and he may have inspired the majority
of his fellow Britons to do likewise, but the method which he
employed for eight or nine years to generate scientific romances on a wholesale basis was taken up by others. Although the British tradition of scientific romance owed more
to the twentieth century Wells than to his nineteenth century
forbear, American science fiction took both its inspiration

and its method from the work which Wells did between 1893 and 1901.

The United States of America had joined the Great War late, and turned out to be its only winner. America, unlike so many European nations, was not threatened by invasion. Although its people suffered some shortages and deprivations, these were nothing like the sufferings of Europe in their scale or their intensity. To cap it all, America inherited the economic hegemony of the world as a result of the destruction of Europe as a financial and industrial hub of world affairs. While Europe struggled to rebuild in the 1920s America enjoyed a spectacular boom, and although Americans had then to agonize along with everyone else when the great Depression of the 1930s followed the Wall Street Crash, there remained an essential optimism in America which contrasted starkly with the urgency of the Age of Frustration which had Britain in its calamitous grip.

By virtue of these different circumstances, the American writers of science fiction discovered a future very different from that discovered by British scientific romance. Most importantly, American science fiction retained its openness, its clear consciousness of a huge range of future alternatives. The vast vistas of space and time which had so excited and inspired the young H. G. Wells came, in later years, to overawe and frighten writers of British scientific romance—to make them aware of the smallness of man and the vanity of human ambition. Even in the future envisaged for humankind in *Last and First Men*, which extends over thousands of millions of years, men do not break out of the cage of interstellar space surrounding the solar system. In American science fiction, by contrast, that bubble was soon and effortlessly pricked, so that the entire galaxy quickly became a playground for pioneers and adventurers.

In American science fiction the world might be threatened by all manner of powerful new weapons, wielded by men or by vicious alien beings, but civilization never trembled on the brink of a bottomless abyss, because there was an indomitable faith in science fiction that human ingenuity could and must prevail. Science fiction writers produced their anxious stories, and even some stories of future worlds

115

from which humans had disappeared, but their tales of terrible hazards and elegiac fantasies of the end of the human story had neither the cynicism nor the urgency of parallel images in British scientific romance. In science fiction, such stories were naive in a good as well as a bad sense of the word. They were usually ill-designed, clumsy, and sketchy in literary terms, but they were also wide-eyed, celebrating the wonder of discovery and extrapolation in a way that British scientific romance very rarely did. Science fiction in the twenties and thirties was mostly facile, but for all its precision, scrupulousness and literary sophistication, British scientific romance had lost something important when it lost its own facility.

The consequence of all this was that in the years immediately following Wells's death, the future was effectively discovered all over again in Britain. The dissolution of British scientific romance into American science fiction was eventually to bring about a fruitful cross-fertilization. All speculative fiction is inherently both serious and playful, but between the wars American science fiction had almost surrendered all claim to seriousness while British scientific romance was crucially inhibited by doubts about the propriety of playfulness. After 1947 speculative fiction in Britain and America began to recover a balance between seriousness and playfulness which permitted them to enter into a synergistic relationship, and this has been greatly to the benefit not only to the literature of speculation but to the flexibility and enterprise of that kind of mindfulness which is orientated towards the future and its opportunities rather than towards the past and its prohibitions.

The achievement of this balance by the best of modern speculative fiction should allow us to appreciate the element of folly in Wells's conversion to the project of discovering an actual and inevitable future instead of a future pregnant with many and varied possibilities. We must remember, though, that such a project is not as entirely ridiculous as fiercer critics than I have made it out to be.

The most scathing of all demolitions of the futurological project actually appeared before Wells delivered his lecture on the discovery of the future: it is to be found in the opening chapter of G. K. Chesterton's futuristic fantasy *The Napoleon of Notting Hill* (1904), which suggests that history is engaged in a never-ending game of "Cheat the Prophet," perversely determined to defy our anticipations with arbitrary shifts. This is untrue. The whole basis of rational thought—the power which makes us human—is our ability to anticipate the probable outcomes of different actions, and thus to choose between them.

What Wells says about the kind of mindfulness which is orientated toward the future is well worth attending to, and he is quite right to suggest that if we insist on being mindful of the future only in a narrow and personal sense then we are guilty of a great cowardice and a great irresponsibility. The fact that we cannot discover by inference a future history which is already mapped out for us does not mean that we should be in any way less mindful of the future, nor does it mean that we have a license to play carelessly with whatever fantastic future scenarios we can make plausible.

* * * * * * *

It is good that many others followed where H. G. Wells led—and it is good that they followed up on both his discoveries of the future, eventually bringing them back together again, reuniting them in the modern genre of post-World War II science fiction. This genre—whose foundations Wells laid twice over—has blossomed into a vast industry, whose imagery has become an intrinsic element of modern popular culture. Dozens of invisible men have followed where the luckles Griffin led; hundreds of ambitious scientists have set out as Dr. Moreau did to remake and remould the flesh which is our natural heritage; thousands of alien invaders have fallen upon the earth like Wells's Martians from the great wilderness of space; tens of thousands of astronauts have set forth like Bedford and Cavor into that same wilderness in search of alien landscapes and alien societies.

H. G. Wells was one of the first men fully to appreciate that if we are careful enough in our reasoning, and bold enough in our vision, we may be able to foresee at least some of the possibilities and threats which lie in wait for us as

SLAVES OF THE DEATH SPIDERS, BY BRIAN STABLEFORD

technology advances and the world changes. Although the
actual shape of things to come is yet to be determined by the
combined effects of our ambitions, our actions and our discoveries, and cannot possibly be determined as would-be
prophets hope to determine it, the investigation of its myriad
its possibilities remains an intellectually worthwhile activity.
It also remains an exciting activity, which carries with it a
very special thrill. That is why Wells's scientific romances
are entitled to be considered highly significant texts—
perhaps more significant than anything else he wrote. By
their example, they helped to promote a new way of looking
at the world, and a new way of thinking about the world.

The invention of a time machine was a bold stroke of
the literary imagination. Wells knew perfectly well, of
course, that the machine was purely and simply a literary
device, incapable of realization, just as he knew perfectly
well that an invisible man would be blind (because light
which passed straight through him would be unable to excite
the retinas of his eyes). He also knew, however, that the real
"time machine" was the human imagination itself, and that if
one had to invoke the image of a machine in order to make
the products of the imagination seem more solidly depend-
able than "mere dreams," such an invocation was entirely
justified.

The possible futures mapped out by the time machine of
the imagination require constant revision and updating to
take in our real discoveries, but it is vitally important in a
world like ours that we never lose sight of them. It is far
more useful to know what might happen than what must
happen, because knowing all the things which might happen
offers us a chance to choose which of those things we want
to happen, and which ones we desperately want to avoid. It
is, in fact, more important to know about the things which
we definitely do not want to happen, but which might if we
cannot take steps avoid them, than it is to know about the
things which we would quite like to happen. We must first of
all avoid destroying ourselves, or allowing ourselves to be
destroyed; only when we have done that can we think sen-
sibly about making the world better. This is why so many of
the futures glimpsed through the time machine of the imagi-

nation are horrible and frightening; their purpose is to frighten us into taking care that we will not let such futures sneak up on us while we are not paying attention.

In the pages of modern science fiction stories, the time machine of the imagination is now operated simultaneously by thousands of writers working in dozens of different languages. It has to be, because as time goes by the pace of change speeds up, and many more possibilities come into view: many more dangers and many more threats, but also many more opportunities. We already know, a mere hundred years after Wells wrote his classic essay, that the future his time traveller saw is a mere phantom which cannot come true. We now know the secrets of the genetic code, and we have every reason to suppose that we will become masters of our own future evolution, and of the evolution of all life on earth.

The great adventure in which our children, and our children's children, will take part, is greater than anything H. G. Wells could imagine; but because he showed us the way to do it, we can imagine it, and we should certainly try as hard as we can to foresee all of its possibilities, good and bad. The future is yet to be made as well as discovered, by ourselves, our children and our children's children. Whatever power of choice we can exercise will depend on the extent and on the cleverness of our mindfulness. For this reason, we must do everything that actually is within our power to do what Wells asked of us, and discover what we can of the futures which are presently vying to be made by the collaborative decisions of contemporary men and women

SLAVES OF THE DEATH SPIDERS, BY BRIAN STABLEFORD

X.

THE MANY RETURNS OF DRACULA

The years leading up to the end of the last century, which brought the Victorian era to a close, produced two literary characters whose names have become more famous than any others and whose careers have extended over the intervening hundred years, quite unaffected by the fact that their creators killed them off and then died themselves.

One of these characters was a perfect hero for his times: a master of deductive reasoning who applied his genius to the unravelling of mysteries and the frustration of evil-doers. The other was an archetype of evil who, although he seemed at first glance to be an anachronism left over from an earlier time, might better be regarded as the perfect incarnation of a quintessentially Victorian paranoia. It is significant, however, that when these polar opposites were eventually brought together in one of the multitudinous exercises in pastiche which extended their adventures, they did not meet as enemies but as collaborators—and the scrupulous author of their joint enterprise took great care to point out that they were so similar in their physical descriptions as to be able to pass for close relatives. The two characters are, of course, Sherlock Holmes and Dracula, and the pastiche in question is *The Holmes-Dracula File* (1978) by Fred Saberhagen.

Unlike Holmes, who featured in four novels and dozens of short stories by his original creator, Dracula was initially featured in a single novel, published in 1897 (although a chapter dropped from the novel, in which the Count does not actually appear, was later published separately as "Dracula's

Guest"). Holmes had the customary elasticity of a hero: he could always be provided with yet another challenge over which he would naturally triumph, and the record of his exploits was inherently endless. Dracula was not in such a fortunate position, because the usual expectation is that a plot should conclude with the villain's destruction; the extension of his adventures was bound to be a much more problematic business—but where there's a will there's a way, and in this particular case the will was determined by Dracula's success in Hollywood. Interested filmmakers had no difficulty at all in finding material for a multitude of Sherlock Holmes films, but they were forced to handle Dracula's cinematic career very differently. Necessity proved, as usual, to be the mother of improvization, and they did what they had to do in their own inimitable fashion.

There are, of course, several different cinema versions of Dracula itself. The four most important are F. W. Murnau's *Nosferatu* (1923), starring Max Schreck; Tod Browning's *Dracula* (1931), starring Bela Lugosi; Terence Fisher's *Horror of Dracula* (1958), starring Christopher Lee; and Francis Coppola's *Bram Stoker's Dracula* (1993), starring Gary Oldman. All of these films, like the book, end with Dracula's destruction. Film-makers were not slow to notice, however, that the manner of his destruction already had an escape-clause built in. Because the count was never really alive it was not inconceivable—nor did it seem particularly unsporting—that he might be restored to "undeath" by some arbitrary imaginative flourish, so that he might be destroyed all over again (and again, and again, and again....). Then again, given his nature and *modus operandi* he could easily be credited with a large family of literal and figurative blood relations, among whom were ultimately to be numbered *Dracula's Daughter* (1936), *Son of Dracula* (1943), *Brides of Dracula* (1960), *Countess Dracula* (1970), and *Dracula's Widow* (1989), not to mention *Blacula* (1972) and *Dracula's Dog* (1978; aka *Zoltan—Hound of Dracula*).

Not unnaturally, this promiscuous artistic license quickly came to seem silly, and the ritualistic repetition of Dracula's rebirth and redestruction contributed in no small measure to the fact that many of his later manifestations reduced the count to a kind of camp joke (a joke which reached its feeblest levels of parody in *The Munsters* and *Sesame Street*). Sufficient charisma was attached to the role to secure Bela Lugosi and Christopher Lee lifelong fame, but that same charisma made it terribly difficult for either of them to play any other character with authority—and although both actors played the part absolutely straight, with considerable conviction, they found themselves damned nevertheless by the camp jokiness associated with other manifestations of the character.

In spite of his cinematic debasement, however, the character of Dracula has retained an earnest aspect. Later users of the figure have frequently attempted to cut through the veils of ludicrousness which have come to enshroud it, in order to rescue the emotional charge which still resides there. The incessant revitalization of Dracula is not, therefore, merely a matter of narrative convenience; it appears that the character of Dracula is strong enough to withstand any amount of ham-fisted treatment and not be irreversibly diminished. For this reason, Dracula continues to weather and transcend the crudity and caricature of much modern treatment, just as easily as he survived the slightly ham-fisted treatment he received from his original creator.

* * * * * *

As with the work with which it is so frequently coupled in the popular imagination, Mary Shelley's *Frankenstein*, the seed of *Dracula* was sown by a dream. While he was alive Bram Stoker referred to this dream rather vaguely as a vision of a "King-Vampire" rising from his grave, and dismissively attributed it to the effect of having dined too well on dressed crab. His extensive working notes, however, make it clear that the scene in the book which is derived from the initial dream—and was the first to be written down—is that which concludes Chapter III. Here, the appearance of the lordly male vampire is a climactic moment, which saves Jonathan Harker, in the nick of time, from the clutches of three female vampires. It is the most intensely erotic passage in the whole book—and not for lack of competition.

SLAVES OF THE DEATH SPIDERS, BY BRIAN STABLEFORD

This revelation has, of course, been a boon to critics fond of dream-interpretation, some of whom have gone so far as to declare that Stoker's dream must have been a guilty transfiguration of an actual visit to a brothel, probably reflecting his awareness of the fact that some such visit had resulted in his infection with syphilis. This interpretation may be too fanciful (the conjecture that Stoker had syphilis is unsubstantiated by any hard evidence, although adherents of Freudian theory tend to think that the subject-matter and fevered manner of his last novel, *The Lair of the White Worm*, are proof enough) but there seems little doubt that the dream which Stoker had was powerfully erotic. It is understandable that he should have felt sufficiently uncomfortable about this to make light of it, but it is also understandable that he should attempt to preserve the experience, and expand upon it, in the relatively safe medium of fiction—in which a careful transmutation of the imagery could serve the censorial purpose that could only be served in conversation by omission.

The manner in which the dream-seed of *Dracula* is elaborated into a full-blown plot is, of course, rather evasive—the three female vampires who feature in this scene do not appear again until they are brusquely staked at the end—but its eroticism is nevertheless conserved. The role which the "King-Vampire" takes on in the novel is that of an evil force aimed directly at the sexual impulses of the other female characters in the book: Lucy Westenra and Mina Murray (who becomes Mina Harker in the course of the plot, but is not thereby immunized against the corruptive seductions of Dracula). The straightforwardly brutal threat which Dracula poses to the male members of the cast is a poor generator of horror by comparison with the threat he poses to the women they adore. The true horror is, of course, that he does not threaten them with death (which becomes, in the context of the plot, a merciful release devoutly to be wished) but with a metamorphic fate literally and metaphorically worse than death. The exact nature of this metamorphosis is very precisely described in Chapter XVI, in which the heroes confront the undead Lucy:

> The sweetness was turned to adamantine,
> heartless cruelty, and the purity to voluptuous
> wantonness...eyes unclean and full of hell-
> fire, instead of the pure, gentle orbs we
> knew...her eyes blazed with unholy light, and
> the face became wreathed with a voluptuous
> smile....[1]

In brief, what has happened is that Dracula's "kiss" (in Stoker, vampires do not bite, they kiss) has transformed Lucy from the Victorian ideal of womanhood into a sexual predator redolent with whorish glamour. The fact that his subsequent attacks on Mina continue in spite of her marriage adds a further dimension of horror to this awful thought.

At this almost-explicit level of symbolism, the text of the novel becomes an agonized rhapsody on the subject of Victorian ideas of sexuality—and Dracula's emergence from the Gothic mists becomes a horror-stricken recognition of the fact that Victorian morality, no matter how strict or how strenuous its denials might be, could not in the end abolish or contain the reality of female sexuality. Given this, it is hardly surprising that Dracula could not long be forced to remain in the grave before getting up again (and again, and again, and again...).

* * * * * * *

Bram Stoker researched the folkloristic background of *Dracula* for seven years, and clearly took the business of nurturing and developing his dream-seed very seriously indeed—but the dream was not the actual point of origin of the project. Like the dream which gave impetus to Mary Shelley's novel, Stoker's nightmare was as much a consequence of his interest in vampirism as a cause of it. The roots of the project went back a long way.

Stoker read J. Sheridan Le Fanu's classic vampire novella "Carmilla" (1872) when he was twenty-five. This was four years before his first meeting with Henry Irving and six years before he married Oscar Wilde's one-time sweetheart Florence Balcombe, mere days after agreeing to take over responsibility for the actor's business affairs. Six further years were to pass before he began to think seriously about the possibility of writing a vampire novel himself, but even so, it was "Carmilla" which shaped his idea of what a vampire story was and ought to be. The first of Stoker's published short stories had appeared in 1872; Le Fanu had then been, and had remained, his most significant literary influence. The two had much in common—both were graduates of Trinity College, Dublin and Le Fanu was proprietor and editor of the *Dublin University Magazine* for many years (he died in 1873). Stoker must also have been familiar with John Polidori's "The Vampyre" (1819), in which a prolific despoiler of young maidens, is revealed in the concluding line (surely to no one's surprise, given the title) to be "a VAMPYRE!" but it was "Carmilla" that he ardently desired to recapitulate. His decision became firmer when his memory of it was sharply jogged in 1890, by certain tales told by a Hungarian professor of languages, Arminius Vambery, when he was a guest at the "Beefsteak Club"—a regular social gathering which Stoker ran in his capacity as Irving's factotum. This was the context in which Stoker was able to understand his dream, and these were the resources he drew upon in developing it.

It was Vambery who provided much of the folkloristic background for Stoker's conceptualization of vampirism, and gave him an initial reading-list of research materials. Later, when Stoker discovered a fifteenth-century warlord on whom he decided to model his King-Vampire—a Voivode whose scribes signed his name in a variety of ways, including "Dracula," but who was better known to history as Vlad Tepes, "the Impaler," by virtue of his expertise in the art of deterrence, initially cultivated while driving out the Turkish invaders of his homeland—he immediately wrote to Vambery for further assistance, which was provided.

This historical and anthropological dressing-up of the King-Vampire figure was, in a sense, a matter of disguising him. This was a necessary process in literary terms, and perhaps it was necessary in psychological terms too, if there is anything at all in the psychoanalytic truism that raw libidinous impulses must be decorously dressed in symbols before the conscious mind can bear to contemplate them. This process of scholarly sublimation still seems to be going on among those most intimately involved with *Dracula*. There is something slightly peculiar about the way in which assiduous researchers like Clive Leatherdale[2] and Radu Florescu[3] have repeated and extended the studies which Stoker carried out, and a suspiciously-inclined Freudian would probably claim that they manifest a degree of obsession beyond what would actually be necessary either to write or to understand the text of *Dracula*—but I shall not pursue this point, lest even I might come to seem guilty by association.

The most remarkable aspect of *Dracula*'s continued success as an image is the way that this disguise has held together in spite of every absurdity added to it by cinematic convention: the opera-cloak, the bloodshot eyes, and—of course—the ludicrous fangs. No matter how fancy the dress, the awareness remains that there is something lurking beneath that is authentically dangerous.

This is surely all the more remarkable when one recalls that the world has changed very considerably since Victorian times. In the late twentieth century the Victorian attempt to portray female nature as something essentially angelic and asexual seems ridiculously stupid and utterly out-of-date...except, of course, that matters of sexuality are never quite as simple and straightforward as that.

The Victorians, were, of course, not short of conspicuous images of what Stoker called "wantonness" and "voluptuousness," although they might have balked at the temerity of one who dared to call herself Madonna. They knew all along that such success as they dared to claim in binding sexuality to a fiercely-repressive morality was ninety per cent pretence. By the same token, we moderns are by no means short of imagery which overtly or covertly takes it for granted that women (unlike men) are—again using Stoker's terms—"sweet," "gentle," and "pure." We too have known all along that the supposed sexual liberation we achieved in the 1960s is ninety per cent pretence, especially in respect of female sexuality. Even feminists, in their laudable haste to occupy the moral high ground, sometimes seem to be crying out, in mocking parody of the saint of old: "Lord, give me unchastity, but please—not yet!"

* * * * * * *

The contemporary boom in vampire stories is to a large extent an exercise in revisionism, in which Dracula's status as an archetype of evil is defiantly challenged. In the most extreme cases, the vampire becomes a valiant hero, whose effect on his female victims is straightforwardly liberating.

Stoker's text is comprehensively turned on its head by Fred Saberhagen's *The Dracula Tape* (1975), where the count explains that all the notional authors of the original novel (which is, of course, presented as a series of documents, mostly penned by Jonathan Harker, Dr. Seward, and Mina) completely misunderstood what was happening. Here, Dracula claims that the man actually responsible for Lucy's death and Mina's illness was Professor van Helsing, who recklessly gave them transfusions without any regard for the niceties of blood-typing, and that his own actions were designed to save them. Saberhagen's story is ingenious both on the literal level, in that it provides an account of the events described in Dracula which makes more sense than Stoker's, and on the psychological level, in that it firmly links the psychological hang-ups of the Victorians to their hopeless ignorance of almost all aspects of human science.

Other heroic vampire stories elaborate this thesis extensively. In Pierre Kast's vividly erotic historical fantasy *The Vampires of Alfama* (1975; tr. 1976) the heroic vampire becomes an embodiment of all the ideals of the Enlightenment, ranged against the oppressive tyranny of Church and State. Chelsea Quinn Yarbro's Comte de Saint-Germain, in the series of novels and stories begun with *Hôtel Transylvania* (1978), is less concerned with matters of science and more Byronically romantic than frankly libertine, but he is just as squarely on the side of right. The second novel in the series, *The Palace* (1979), pits the count against the malevolent religious fundamentalism of Savonarola in Renaissance Florence, while *Blood Games* (1979) recalls the days of Nero's Rome, and *Tempting Fate* (1982) brings him into the twentieth century to the world of the Russian revolution and the rise of Nazism.

It did not take long for the vampire to colonize other heroic roles. In the later novels in Saberhagen's series, following his fruitful meeting with his great contemporary, he becomes enmeshed in conventional thriller plots. P. N. Elrod's "Vampire Files" (opened 1990) feature a hard-boiled vampire private-eye. In numerous stories of these kinds—most notably Freda Warrington's *A Taste of Blood Wine* (1992)—heroic vampires must face adversaries of their own kind, thus becoming doubly Byronic, in their defiant alienation as well as their seductive charm. Such works as these have not entirely displaced the traditional imagery, but they have assisted in its transformation into something far more ironic. In Kim Newman's luridly extravagant *Anno Dracula* (1992), the melancholy nice vampires are completely overshadowed by the flamboyantly nasty ones, led by an uncompromisingly monstrous Dracula, now married to Queen Victoria (whom he keeps on a leash).

The most successful revisionist vampire stories of modern times are, of course, those of Anne Rice, begun with *Interview with the Vampire* (1976). These walk an anti-heroic tightrope between traditional and revisionist imagery, trading heavily on the moral uncertainties of their leading characters, who experience their own peculiar existential angst and worry endlessly about the dubious relevance to themselves of various moral philosophies. Similar issues are brought more tightly into focus by Suzy McKee Charnas's analytically-inclined fix-up novel *The Vampire Tapestry* (1980), but Rice's escalation of such hypothetical anxieties into fevered melodrama is perhaps more appropriate to the handling of materials which still retain their disguised emotional potency. My own vampire novels, *The Empire of Fear* (1988) and *Young Blood* (1992), attempt something similar.

The phenomenon constituted by this proliferation of vampires—all of whom are parasitic upon the work done by Bram Stoker—is quite astonishing. Why these myriad hares should suddenly have started to run in the mid-1970s, and why their running should have inspired so very many exercises in imitation and extrapolation, is by no means clear, although this was certainly the period in which all manner of social accountants began adding up and evaluating the achievements of the sexually-liberating evolutions and revolutions of the 1960s. Although she was a decade ahead of her time, the real pioneer of vampire revisionism was Jane Gaskell, in whose novel *The Shiny Narrow Grin* (1964) a conspicuously trendy heroine took a typically laid-back attitude to a vampire in modern dress. The moral ironies of Gaskell's novel contrast strikingly with the calculated confusions of Simon Raven's equally knowing but far more traditional *Doctors Wear Scarlet*, published four years earlier.

Raven's novel is one of the few twentieth-century stories which attempt to rescue the pre-Stoker tradition of literary vampirism, which took its inspiration from Classical sources and which almost invariably featured female vampires who needed no King-Vampire to create and discipline them. The most famous English examples, apart from "Carmilla," are Coleridge's "Christabel" (1816) and Keats' "Lamia" (1820), but the German Romantic movement produced earlier examples on which these are partly based, and nineteenth-century French literature is particularly rich in female vampires, the most familiar being Clarimonde in Gautier's "La Morte amoureuse" (1836). The lush eroticism of these works pays equal homage, in its way, to the colorful paradoxicality of male sexual fantasy, but there is no doubt that Dracula somehow adds in an extra element which they lack. *Femmes fatales*, seen in isolation, are often tragic figures—Keats's "Lamia" brings sentimentality to the fore, and some such sympathy is usually latent in other works of this kind—but the evocation of the King-Vampire who manufactures them wholesale (and almost invariably abandons them to death or summary impalement) adds an extra turn of the screw by which the pathos of their fate only serves to generate further horror.

This observation raises again the question of what it is which lurks within Dracula's disguise. So far we have only answered this with an analysis of what he does, but to say that he symbolizes the force of female sexuality which threatens to transform innocent maidens into voluptuous wantons is at best only half an explanation. Connecting all the blood-imagery in vampire stories to the phenomenon of menstruation, as the editors of the recent Creation Press anthology *Blood and Roses* (1992) extravagantly do, adds one more facet but can hardly be said to complete the task.

It is noticeable that both *Dracula* and his closest literary ancestor can be linked—tentatively, at least—with real people. Polidori's lurid depiction of Lord Ruthven clearly owes much to his temporary association with Lord Byron, and Stoker's image of Dracula surely draws on his relationship with Henry Irving, whose personality so overwhelmed him on the days following their first meeting that he eventually made Irving's service his primary vocation. In this context the Count's jealous reaction to discovering Jonathan Harker with the three female vampires, at the end of the sequence based on Stoker's dream, is of some interest. "Never did I imagine such fury, even in the demons of the pit," Harker says—and yet Dracula subsequently seems to lose all interest in him, facilitating his unlikely escape by careless neglect, and much prefers other prey when they eventually meet up again.

Some psychoanalytically-inclined commentators have interpreted the attitudes of both Polidori and Stoker in terms of repressed homosexuality, but a simpler explanation—and it is sometimes unwise to ignore the obvious in favor of the occult—is that they looked upon their idols with pure and simple envy. In the former instance at least, this interpretation is supported by a famous anecdote which relates how Polidori attempted to swallow poison after asking what Byron could do better than he and receiving a blunt and accurate answer.

If this is true, the mystery of *Dracula*'s symbolism—and of his awesome, enduring power—is not so very difficult to unwrap. Dracula becomes, in this analysis, an embodiment of male fears of inadequacy, especially in the face of female sexuality. It is not simply the fact that Dracula can turn the most demure virgin into an avid sex maniac that is important, but the fact that other men can't. That, for the book's author and the vast majority of its readers, might be the true horror—the ultimate horror—which can survive any amount of disguise and obfuscation.

SLAVES OF THE DEATH SPIDERS, BY BRIAN STABLEFORD

Is this why *Dracula*, in spite of all the ridicule that Hollywood and generations of (male) comedians heaped upon him, retains the power to disturb and remains a threat? Is it because, no matter how men strive to cover up their feelings of inadequacy with lewd jokes and lurid erotic obsessions, the gnawing anxiety will always remain? Perhaps, though, I ought not to pursue this point, lest even I should come to seem guilty by association....

XI.

TARZAN'S DIVIDED SELF

In Chapter Fourteen of *Tarzan of the Apes* by Edgar Rice Burroughs, the English nobleman William Cecil Clayton, who has gone astray in "the twilight depths of the African jungle," finds himself face to face with a hungry lion. His end seems nigh, but hurtling to his rescue comes the remarkable person he has ever seen: a man who is "the embodiment of physical perfection and giant strength." The stranger, armed only with a knife, wrestles and kills the lion, then stands erect over its carcase and lets loose a bloodcurdling cry of feral triumph.

This extraordinary event is even more melodramatic than the bare facts indicate. William Clayton does not know, and does not find out in the course of the novel—although the reader has known all along—that this magnificent creature is in fact his cousin, and the rightful heir to the title which he believes to be his own! Thanks to a miraculously fortunate admixture of genetic and environmental influences Tarzan of the Apes is, in a perfectly literal sense, the epitome of the Noble Savage.

Tarzan of the Apes was first published in the October 1912 issue of *The All-Story Magazine*, and was an instant hit. By the time it appeared in book form its author had already produced a sequel, *The Return of Tarzan*, and he went on to answer popular demand by issuing more than twenty more. Burroughs was ultimately to found his own publishing company to package his own works, and he registered the name "Tarzan" as a trademark. By such means he became the first man ever to make a million dollars writing popular fiction. Burroughs wrote other popular series of novels, including one set on Mars and another on the inner surface of the supposedly-hollow earth, but the foundation-stone of his success was the character of Tarzan, who became one of that select handful of fictional individuals—the others include Scrooge, Sherlock Holmes, and Dracula—whose names are universally familiar to everyone, even to people who have never read any of the books in which they appear.

Tarzan's career soon overflowed the print medium, extending into a long series of films, the first of which was released in 1932, and a plethora of comic strips. This extension is a remarkable feat, because—unlike Sherlock Holmes, who could be confronted with an infinite supply of unique puzzles to unravel—Tarzan is a character of rather limited scope. His original creator soon began to find it difficult to think of new things for him to do; there were plenty more lions to vanquish, but killing them quickly became a perfunctory ritual, and it is unsurprising that having run the customary gamut of damsels in distress, sneering villains, cannibal tribesmen, and lost cities, Burroughs's plotting strategies became increasingly desperate. He dabbled in the bizarre in such novels as *Tarzan and the Ant Men* (1924) and *Tarzan at the Earth's Core* (1930), and he resorted to satire in *Tarzan and the Lion Man* (1934)—in which he derided the film *Tarzan*, whom he considered to be an insulting travesty of the character he created—but in the end he virtually gave up, and the series decayed into enfeebled exercises in self-plagiarism. (One of the later novels, *Tarzan and the Forbidden City* [1938], was obviously ghost-written, by someone who seems not to have bothered to study the originals he was meant to be imitating.) Despite such difficulties, though, Tarzan's career continued long after Burroughs's death, and would have proliferated even more promiscuously had the Burroughs estate not been so conscientious in taking legal action against pirates who borrowed the character without permission.

Attempts by other writers to imitate the Tarzan novels are numerous, and there has grown up a whole sub-genre of adventure stories about feral children raised to near-superhumanity by tigers, leopards, bears and (most recently, in Nicholas Luard's 1990 novel *Kala*) hyenas. Burroughs other books have been even more widely imitated, especially the series of interplanetary adventures which he initiated with his first novel, *A Princess of Mars* (1912 as "Under the Moons of Mars"; in book form 1917), but this is largely because these other novels have offered more imaginative scope to imitators—the exotic settings allow the introduction of an infinite variety of grotesquely monstrous enemies to be overcome by the athletic heroes. It is arguable that Burroughs' most interesting works are his more imaginatively daring forays into science fiction—especially the two trilogies collected as *The Land That Time Forgot* (1918; in book form 1924) and *The Moon Maid* (1923-25; in book form 1926)—and it is not surprising that these works still have a cult following. However, it is Tarzan who is the one figure of mythical dimension in the Burroughs canon, and the mystery which must be unravelled if Burroughs's success is to be understood.

* * * * * * *

In *Tarzan of the Apes* John Clayton, heir apparent to the title of Lord Greystoke, is cast away with his new bride on the coat of equatorial West Africa, following a mutiny aboard their yacht. They are presumed dead, and eventually do die, but their baby son is adopted by Kala, a female of an imaginary protohuman species of ape, whose own infant has been killed by the "king" of her "tribe."

In order to survive in this harsh milieu John Clayton Jr. must cultivate greater bodily strength and fighting skill than his adoptive kindred, and he eventually develops such supremacy that he is able to kill the king and take his place. His superior intelligence allows him to learn the use of weapons without instruction or example. He also learns to read and write (but not to speak) English from the books left behind in his parents' ramshackle hut.

Tarzan's adoptive tribe has human neighbors, but are not on good terms with them, and the difference in his skin color prevents him identifying with them; it is not until he is twenty years old that Tarzan encounters other white men, who are marooned exactly as he was. This party consists of an American antiquarian, Archimedes Q. Porter, his daughter Jane and her maid, his assistant, and William Clayton.

These newcomers fail dismally—and rather farcically—to cope with the wilderness, and Tarzan becomes their secret benefactor, watching over them and saving their lives whenever necessary. He falls in love with Jane after rescuing her from one of his adoptive cousins, who attempts to rape her, but understandable difficulties in communication prevent him from finding out that his feelings are reciprocated, and he wrongly concludes that she is in love with Clayton.

Eventually, the new castaways are rescued by French soldiers, who are forced to abandon their commander, Paul D'Arnot, when he is carried off by cannibals. Tarzan rescues D'Arnot, and learns a great deal from him—including the French language—while nursing him back to health. D'Arnot, meanwhile, deduces Tarzan's true identity from the contents of the hut. D'Arnot escorts Tarzan to the civilized world, and while the Frenchman sets out to prove that he is the true Lord Greystoke, Tarzan goes to America in search of Jane.

Tarzan finds Jane in dire straits, about to be reluctantly married off to a wicked financier to whom her father owes money, but he contrives to save her from this sad fate, and from a forest fire. He is, however, still laboring under the delusion that Jane loves William Clayton, and when he receives a telegram confirming that he is the true heir to the Greystoke title, he decides that honor compels him discreetly to disappear, leaving both the title and the girl to his cousin.

The Return of Tarzan follows the consequences of this unparalleled *beau geste*. Tarzan lives for a while in Paris, but he discovers that civilization is too insipid and hypocritical for his unrefined tastes, and is glad to embark upon a career as a secret agent. While he is *en route* to South Africa, a chance meeting with Jane's best friend allows him to discover his mistake in thinking that Jane loved his cousin, but he is thrown overboard by his enemies before being able to do anything about it. Not until he has completed a further series of jungle adventures—in the course of which he becomes the chief of the Waziri tribe and discovers the lost city of Opar—can he locate Jane again. Even then he must take care of his civilized enemies, and overcome further difficulties and misunderstandings before finally marrying her.

Only one other book in the series, *The Son of Tarzan* (1917), really carries Tarzan's life story forward to any significant degree. *Jungle Tales of Tarzan* (1919) fills in details of his early life omitted from *Tarzan of the Apes*, but the remainder are repetitive accounts of formulaic adventures which simply constitute a series of footnotes to the story told in the first two volumes. The core of the true Tarzan myth ("true" in the sense that the grunting, liana-swinging, crocodile-wrestling paragon of inarticulacy portrayed in the early films is, as Burroughs thought, a mere travesty) is to be found entire in the first two books of the series—and there is a case to be made that it really resides in the first alone.

* * * * * * *

Tarzan is, essentially, a creature of two worlds. He is a jungle predator who stalks his prey, kills it—with his bare hands if necessary—and eats it raw. Other animal predators are his respected rivals, and despite his awesome physique it is his intelligence which gives him the edge over them. His ability to reason is superior to their inborn instincts, and his own instincts are those of an idealized English nobleman: he is by nature gallant, chivalrous and dutiful. It is, however, precisely these noble instincts which lead him to despise the world of civilized men.

However paradoxical it may seem, it is Tarzan's harsh upbringing in a world of nature red in tooth and claw which has allowed his instinctive nobility to flourish. Human "predators" he despises, because their motives for killing seem to him to be dishonest and perverted. It seems to Tarzan that like William Clayton, but in most cases infinitely more so, the vast majority of men are unentitled to their inheritance; they have, ironically, been brutalized by their insulation from the law of the jungle.

In Tarzan's world-view, the violence of the jungle is entirely legitimate; in the jungle one has to kill to eat, and one must fight other predators for the privilege, and that is what one does. The violence of civilized men, by contrast, is a kind of sickness, based in oppression, deceit and naked sadism. Tarzan can find no authentic morality in the world of civilized men, where competition in the interests of survival has been overtaken by competition for money, whose principal use is "to purchase the effeminate pleasures of weaklings." He can see little moral difference between the great majority of black men (whom he considers to be superstitious cannibals) and the great majority of white men (who seem to him to be greedy hypocrites), and even that minority of men—black or white—which stands above the general run of their kind has its superior counterpart in the animal world, in species like the elephant and certain rare individuals like Jad-bal-ja the Golden Lion.

It scarcely needs to be emphasized that Tarzan's jungle bears very little resemblance to the actual African rain forest, ecologically speaking. Many of the animals featured in *Tarzan of the Apes* (including lions) are not forest-dwellers, and the apes which play such a vital role are entirely imaginary. The author's version of the novel also featured tigers, though this proved a little too much for the copy-editor, who removed them. Tarzan's jungle is a purely hypothetical construct: a primeval state of nature inhabited by archetypal symbols (thus, each species has its identifying name: Numa the Lion, Tantor the Elephant, etc.) If we are to make sense of this we can only do so in psychological terms; matters of narrative realism do not enter into it.

Tarzan of the Apes is a curious celebration of Rousseauesque ideas about the nobility of savagery and the idea that a fundamentally virtuous human nature is routinely spoiled and perverted by cultural artifice. As a parable of the power of innocence, it has a considerable appeal to those individuals who feel most acutely the manifold constraints and petty injustices of life in civilized society. Many of those most afflicted by such stress are children, but anyone can identify with Tarzan who has felt the weariness of conformity with social norms and the frustrations of confrontation with cultural complexity. Tarzan is, however, more than just a mighty barbarian licensed by circumstance to do all the things we are physically and circumstantially prevented from doing; he has a wholeness which we have not. He has the heart of a lion and the mind of an aristocrat, and the two are not in conflict. In him, emotion and intellect, appetite and self-control, id and superego, are in perfect harmony. If he is out of place in high society, that is only because high society is not worthy of him; he is at home in the jungle not because he is bestial but because he is strong enough to subject the jungle to his ennobling influence, in becoming its rightful and acknowledged king.

The most lyrical passages in the Tarzan books describe the moments when Tarzan comes home to the jungle after a time in the civilized world, and celebrates his release. There is a similar critical moment in *The Son of Tarzan*, when Tarzan's son—who has been brought up to be properly civilized—is forced by circumstance to discover his true self in that same jungle. This is the ultimate liberation which the Tarzan books offer their readers: not simply the joy of casting off all the shackles of civilization, but the promise that when that is done, you will find yourself at home. Perhaps Tarzan's jungle is a perverse Utopia, but it is a Utopia nevertheless. It is a turbulent Garden of Eden where the lion will never lie down with the lamb, nor can he ever be expected to, but it is a kind of Eden. It is a paradise for the adventurous, who would be bored to tears in Heaven.

Many adults would deem this a childish idea, and it is perfectly understandable that no one but a child is likely to be sufficiently unselfconscious to confess that his idea of the good life involves the freedom to slaughter human and animal villains on a massive scale. If we were honest, though, there would probably be few among us who could claim to be entirely unafflicted by fantasies of doing violence—often extreme and ingenious violence—to those who annoy and frustrate us in the thousand trivial ways which everyday life permits and necessitates.

It is partly because *Tarzan of the Apes* offers us this kind of gratification in an unashamedly straightforward fashion that Tarzan has won his privileged place among modern hero-myths. But our recognition of the Tarzanic dreams which lurk within us is not without irony, as British satirists knew very well when they employed "Tarzan" as a mocking nickname for the politician Michael Heseltine—whose entitlement to it may, in the end, have been what dissuaded his fellow MPs from electing him their leader. Nor is this irony absent from the books, which recognize and try to deal with it. The ironic dimension shows up most clearly in Tarzan's problematic relationship with Jane.

Jane, as befits a modest heroine cooked up according to the conventional recipe of her day, is a civilizing influence on her husband. She threatens to enmesh him in a net of domesticity and tame him. In most melodramas, this is seen as a suitable fate for a hero, or at least a suitable end for a book, but it is clearly not right for Tarzan, nor for a series of more than twenty books. After their marriage, Tarzan does his best to live with Jane in London, making relatively infrequent returns to his true home, but the conflict of interest between them quickly becomes exposed when their son Jack begins to show signs that he is a chip off the old block. Jane tries to stamp out these atavistic tendencies, but is thwarted—Jack's eventual escape from his false home to his true one is a triumph, and amply demonstrates to Tarzan the folly of allowing himself to be tamed. The family moves to Africa, but this is only a partial solution to the problem.

In *Tarzan and the Jewels of Opar* (1918) Burroughs afflicts Tarzan with amnesia so that he can revert fully to type, but this was not a solution which could be extended indefinitely. Burroughs must have realized by then what the pressure of melodramatic convention had presumably prevented him from realising before—that the end of *Tarzan of the Apes*, far from being a natural lead-in to a sequel, was in fact a perfect conclusion: Jane should indeed have been left to the weak-kneed cousin, while the true hero remained married to his jungle.

In order to solve this problem Burroughs initially took the courageous course; in the magazine serial which became the first half of *Tarzan the Untamed* (1920) he simply killed Jane off. He relented of this harsh decision, however, and brought her back to life in the book version; it is not entirely clear whether this was because his courage failed him in the face of the awesome might of literary convention or because he realized that a Jane who had been carried off, but not killed, could have an entire novel (*Tarzan the Terrible*, 1921) devoted to her recovery.

The problem of what to do with Jane hung over the remainder of the series. In *Tarzan's Quest* (1936) he experimented with the possibility of elevating her to heroic status, allowing her to function as a substitute in much the same way that her offspring had been allowed to come into his heritage in *The Son of Tarzan*, but this was distinctly unconvincing and hardly in the spirit of the overarching enterprise. The alternative solution which Burroughs found to the threat which Jane posed to his otherwise invincible hero was infinitely preferable: in almost all the adventures chronicled after *Tarzan the Terrible* he virtually ignored her, remaining mindful of her existence while ruthlessly excluding her physical presence.

This was the best possible solution to the dilemma which Jane's existence posed. Jane's death might have allowed Tarzan to be tempted again, but while she was permanently present—although conveniently left offstage—the question of Tarzan being ensnared by sexual attraction simply could not arise. This was doubly convenient. Tarzan is the kind of hero who must, indeed, remain "untamed" and "terrible." In a different era he might—like modern haunters of urban wildernesses who are "licensed to kill"—have been prodigiously promiscuous, but given the attitude of his time he was far better off being safely married to an absentee wife, honor-bound to be utterly chaste.

Philip José Farmer, whose *Tarzan Alive* (1972) offers a "corrected" biography of a person whose career was allegedly misreported by Burroughs, tried to adapt his character to the modern formula, but it is by no means clear that such a move was necessary or desirable. A plethora of loveless sex is not particularly attractive, and as a narrative device it quickly becomes as boringly ritualistic as slaughtering lions. It is not surprising that Farmer's own Tarzan pastiches were initially produced as exercises in pornography (although one of them, *Lord of the Trees*, was eventually published—in a rather slim edition—in a version from which all the sex scenes had been carefully excised).

It is not simply the fact that Tarzan was the product of a sexually-inhibited era that makes his innocence appropriate. One can readily see, in retrospect, that he never should have tried to "grow up" at all; his closest literary relative is not Kipling's Mowgli, whose task is to be educated in spite of his peculiar circumstances, but J. M. Barrie's Peter Pan. It was a mistake for Tarzan to take Jane back from his effete cousin, but it was also a mistake for him to try to set up home in Paris and become a secret agent. His one and only true home was his jungle Never Land, and as Peter Pan found out at the end of the novel version of his career, *Peter and Wendy* (1911)—there was nothing for one such as he within the borders of the real world but tragic disillusionment. Even the most determined popular fiction always has to recognize, in the end, that in the real world, uncompromised nobility cannot hold a candle to hypocrisy.

At one point in *The Return of Tarzan* Burroughs states explicitly that to be a child or a primeval man is "the same thing in a way," and that Tarzan is both. This opinion, outdated now, is consonant with the thinking of many early anthropologists, who tried to account for the "primitiveness" of alien cultures by likening their ways of thought to those of children—a view wholeheartedly endorsed by Freud in *Totem and Taboo* (1913). Burroughs is content to differ from all these contemporaries—even, and especially, from Barrie—in seeing nothing incomplete in Tarzan's situation. Tarzan is not a case of arrested development: he is the authentic, whole man; it is those who have gone on to maturity who have become fragmented, as he nearly does himself.

This image of the ideal man recurs in other Burroughs novels, ranging from the offbeat romance of *The Eternal Lover* (1914-15; in book form 1925) to the playful comedy of *The Cave Girl* (1913-17; in book form 1925). It is the condition to which all his heroes tacitly aspire, even though they may not be aware of it themselves. Nor is this an implicitly masculine ideal, despite the implication of such exercises in role-reversal as H. M. E. Clamp's *Wild Cat* (1935), in which the feral woman is condemned by an unthinking author to that hideous fate-worse-than-death which is reserved for the heroines of popular romantic fiction. True female Tarzans can be found in Burroughs's *The Cave Girl* and in S. Fowler Wright's *The Island of Captain Sparrow* (1928) and *Dream; or, The Simian Maid* (1931).

This image of innocent wholeness is, of course, quite false. *Tarzan of the Apes* is a bare-faced lie, from beginning to end—but Burroughs's genius as a writer of popular fiction lay in the realisation that it is not necessary for a writer to pretend too much, and that readers are capable of being grateful for the kind of sincerity which goes straight to the heart of their nostalgic daydreams.

We are all condemned to live in a world whose moral and material imperfections are manifest, and where honesty is—let's face it—the second best policy. Why should we be ashamed to deal with bold and naked lies, if they offer us a vision of a way of being which not only licenses all the impulses which civilized society necessarily and rightly demands that we should suppress, but insists that we would be better and happier people were we fortunate enough to enjoy that way of being?

Tarzan of the Apes is the purest kind of romance there is, because it is one of the few novels which does not pretend that romance must, in the end, be accommodated to social institutions. Its big lie leads us not to the counterfeit ecstasy of wealth and marriage, but to the true ecstasy of being the rightful king of the jungle. It leads us, admittedly, no-where—"nowhere" is, after all, what Utopia means—but it really is useful to have such a destination available.

The tide of literary fashion has now brought us back to an era when it is vey difficult indeed to get to nowhere from here and now but that is a state of affairs which is not entirely to be welcomed.

SLAVES OF THE DEATH SPIDERS, BY BRIAN STABLEFORD

XII.

SYMPATHY FOR THE DEVIL

Jacques Cazotte's *The Devil in Love*

Modern fiction is not short of sympathy for the devil. A rich tradition of literary Satanism has extended from the brief manifesto included in Shelley's *Defence of Poetry* (written 1821, published 1840), which argues that the rebel angel was morally superior to the tyrant God. Numerous infernal comedies have suggested that Hell might not be such a bad place after all, given the interesting company to be found there. Countless deal-with-the-devil stories which accept the malevolent nature of the devil nevertheless make him an urbane and witty fellow, fit company for social occasions if not a safe custodian of immortal souls. All of this work was, however, preceded by Jacques Cazotte's *Le Diable amoureux* (1772), usually known in English as *The Devil in Love*, which is all the more remarkable for its appearance—and great popularity—in a Catholic country whose *ancien régime* had not yet been disturbed by revolution.

Le Diable amoureux tells the story of an unwary young soldier seduced into the employment of magic, who conjures up the devil in the form of a lovely young woman. He falls in love with her, thus preparing the way for his damnation. Summarized in that fashion, the tale could easily pass for a conventional moral tale warning against the horrid cunning of the devil's temptations, and perhaps that is the way that its author planned it, but its development includes a crucial extra twist, which is that the devil—seemingly, a least—enters

145

into the guise of the charming Biondetta so wholeheartedly as to fall in love with the young man "she" has come to tempt.

Although the title of the novel can be read as "the amorous devil" the story does indeed come to seem like a tale of "the devil in love"—and love is a humanizing emotion, at least in fiction. Cazotte's besotted devil is, in fact, a far better candidate for sympathy than the noble rebel appointed by Shelley's successors to be a shining example to all enemies of Divine Tyranny. Even a moralist as strict as Marie Corelli—who was very definitely on the side of those angels loyal to God—was able to find sympathy for a devil who was capable of falling in love, as she did in *The Sorrows of Satan* (1895).

The imaginative step by means of which Cazotte's devil reciprocates the love which "she" sets out to induce is not a vast one, but it is a highly significant one. It may even qualify as a daring one, in that it clearly flirts with heresy, and perhaps with blasphemy—and yet the novel was very widely read and greatly applauded. The story's remarkable inventiveness was thus compounded by its reception, adding to the puzzle of how it came to be produced at all.

In order to understand how this all came about, it is necessary to give detailed consideration to the story's origins: to the particular circumstances of its author, and to the literary currents which had caught him up. These were the key components of the intellectual climate which first gave birth to sympathy for the scapegoat who had been invented and designed to serve as the embodiment of all that was vile and vicious.

* * * * * * *

Jacques Cazotte was born in Dijon in 1719 and educated at the local Jesuit College. There he was extensively schooled in ancient and modern languages, in order to prepare him for a career in foreign affairs. He subsequently studied law, qualifying in 1740. Shortly thereafter he went to Paris in order to enter the Marine Department of the civil service. He was then required by the Minister of Marine to spend a further two years studying marine law in Paris.

While he was pursuing these further studies Cazotte became a member of one of the capital's many literary salons and produced his earliest literary works, *La Patte du chat* (1741) and *Les Mille et une fadaises* (1742; tr. as *A Thousand and One Follies*). Once he had taken up his official duties, however, he found himself fully occupied. He held various posts on shore and aboard ship, and was involved in various naval campaigns against the English during the War of the Austrian Succession.

After being promoted to *écrivain principal* in 1747 Cazotte was posted to the island of Martinique in the Caribbean. There he had an extremely uncomfortable time, continually dogged by poor health and financial difficulties. He seems to have been very badly treated by his superiors and never received the full remuneration due to him for his services, but in 1752 he was recalled to France in order to recover his health and produce a report on the state of the colony. He was drawn once again into the literary life of Paris, producing a few ballads and contributing two pamphlets to the controversy that was then raging regarding the alleged inferiority of French Operatic music to Italian. Cazotte took up the cause of French music, most notably in a vituperative reply to a critical pamphlet issued by Rousseau.

Cazotte returned to Martinique in 1754 but fared no better than before; his health deteriorated again and the hostility of his superiors was renewed. His awkward situation was further complicated by the outbreak of the Seven Years' War, during which the British tried unsuccessfully to capture Martinique. After being partially blinded by scurvy, Cazotte again returned to France in 1759, but was unfortunate enough to attempt to liquidate his assets by handing them over to a Jesuit Mission in exchange for notes of credit payable by the Society in France. These notes turned out to be virtually worthless, because the Mission's credit was already over-extended (although the refusal of the Society to honor them added to the burden of disrepute which eventually led to the suppression of the French Jesuits in 1764).

Cazotte's financial troubles were compounded by the fact that the Ministry of Marine would not offer him an adequate pension following his premature retirement. He would have been in a parlous state had he not inherited from his brother—who, being a clergyman, had no children—a large house in Pierry, near Epernay. Here Cazotte stayed for the remainder of his life. Shortly after taking up residence there he married the daughter of an officer he had known in Martinique, and the couple had three children.

* * * * * * *

It was while living quietly at Pierry, at some distance from but not completely out of touch with the literary world of Paris, that Cazotte wrote his most considerable works. He developed the substance of one of his ballads into the longest of his works, *Ollivier* (1763), a burlesque of the chivalric romances which had flattered and delighted the feudal barons of Medieval France. It was a success with the public in spite of the scorn heaped upon it by unkind critics. This was followed in 1767 by a comic novel, *Le Lord impromptu* (tr. as *His Most Unlooked-For Lordship*), and in 1772—although it may have been written as many as eight years earlier—by his most famous work, *Le Diable amoureux*.

In addition to these three long works Cazotte produced numerous minor pieces, of which several are of some note. *La Nouvelle Raméide* (1766) is a curious "sequel" to a eulogistic poem issued in the same year by Jean-François Rameau, the nephew of a famous composer, whose eccentricities were later to be immortalized by Diderot in *Le Neveu de Rameau* (written 1761; published 1823; tr. as *Rameau's Nephew*). In the same period Cazotte dabbled in the production of fables, after the fashion of La Fontaine. These were later collected in 1788 along with various other items, including "La Belle par accident," a Quixotic fairy tale in the same vein as his earliest publications, and "Rachel" (1788), a new version of a Spanish legend. Cazotte's last major work was a series of Oriental tales—some of them based in authentic Arabian folklore—issued as a *Continuation des mille et une nuits* (1788-89; tr. as *Arabian Tales*).

Cazotte's interest in the fantastic and the occult, exhibited in almost all his literary works, extended in the latter part of his life to a close involvement with the Martinists, an Illuminist sect claiming affiliation to the Rosicrucian Order and Weishaupt's Bavarian Illuminati. The founder of the sect, Martinez de Pasqualis, had established a series of quasi-Masonic lodges in various French cities during the 1760s; after his death in 1768 he was succeeded by the self-styled Saint-Martin, whose close associate Madame la Croix became a member of Cazotte's household, collaborating with him in séances and other occult experiments (somewhat to the discomfort of Mme. Cazotte). It is not clear exactly when Cazotte was initiated into the Order, but the occult apparatus of *Le Diable amoureux* is certainly not taken seriously, and it is not until the Oriental tales written in the late 1780s that the inspiration of Martinist ideas becomes obvious in the author's work.

Cazotte did not remain within the Martinist fold for long; he broke with Saint-Martin in 1789 because the latter favored the revolutionists while Cazotte himself remained steadfastly loyal to the king. In fact, Cazotte's loyalty went so far as to encourage him to draw up plans for a hypothetical counter-revolution, which he laid out in letters to an old friend who was an assistant to Laporte, the controller of the Civil List. When Laporte was arrested and his papers seized these letters fell into the hands of the revolutionists and Cazotte was promptly arrested, along with his daughter Élisabeth. They were imprisoned in the Abbaye Saint-Germain-des-Prés, and although they survived a massacre mounted by the Marsellais Cazotte was brought before a revolutionary tribunal, condemned to death, and guillotined in September 1792.

* * * * * * *

Cazotte's literary work exemplifies many of the popular literary fashions of his day. All of it was written to amuse, and the greater part of it is tongue-in-cheek. Although he was presumably grateful for the money earned by *Le Diable amoureux* and the Oriental tales, there was never any sign of

149

burgeoning professionalism in his career; he remained an amateur throughout. He never laid claim to any considerable talent or artistry, and most of his critics have agreed with his modest stimation of is capability. Even *Le Diable amoureux*, which is universally considered to be his masterpiece, is something of a curate's egg, brilliant in some respects but distinctly ham-fisted in others. Appropriate assessment of the work is not helped by the fact that the extant text appears to be only half the work which Cazotte originally planned. Whether he actually wrote any more is unclear, but the story's ending was certainly rewritten because the first version was deemed unsatisfactory by readers of the first edition.

In spite of these reservations it must be asserted that Cazotte is a key figure in the development of modern fantastic fiction and one of the most important of its founding fathers. He was active in an age when the fantastic materials of oral tradition were first being exploited by *littérateurs*, not in a purely imitative fashion but in an exploratory spirit. He was one of the pioneers who demonstrated that ideas of the supernatural which were incapable of sustaining real belief (his conversion to Martinism cannot be seen as a redemption of the notions deployed in his fiction) were more useful to the writer of amusing, satirical and moralistic fictions than those which can. *Le Diable amoureux* is by far his most important work because it proved, in a particularly audacious fashion, that literary dealings with a metaphorical devil can offer a commentary on the tribulations of temptation far more pointed than any pietistic sermon.

* * * * * * *

Cazotte's earliest stories reflect the fashionability in early eighteenth century France of the remade folktale. Although Charles Perrault initially issued his collection of *Contes de ma mère Loye* (1697; tr. as *Tales of Mother Goose* and many other titles) under his son's name in order to protect his reputation the book took the salons of Paris by storm, and inspired dozens of further collections of *contes de fées*, many of them written by aristocratic ladies or clergymen.

Perrault's stories had all been based on traditional tales, reshaped to sustain the moral lessons which were scrupulously appended to them, but those who followed in his footsteps made little or no distinction between original and borrowed materials. Within a few years fairies were popping up in heavily ironic tales of the contemporary French court, adding an element of burlesque which excused but did not blunt the cutting edge of the satire.

The license which the deployment of fairies gave to writers was by no means confined to satire. The presence of such elements within a story also defused charges of indecency. Galland's translation of the classic anthology of Arabian folktales, the *Mille et une Nuits* (1704-17), not only introduced Oriental elements into the genre but also gave a healthy boost to its eroticism. The satirical irony of the newly-composed tales lent itself very readily to fusion with flirtatiously licentious material, and the importation of such an element did no harm at all to the popularity of such tales in Parisian salons. The French *haut monde* agreed—as if it were entirely obvious—that such tales were mere literary confections, and that they should in consequence allowed a latitude which was not yet to be extended to more seriously-inclined work.

Inevitably, the Orientalized fairy tale was itself satirized, most notably by Antoine Hamilton, although Hamilton's most famous work, and the only one to be translated into English—*Les Quatre Facardins* (1710-15)—remained incomplete. It is not surprising that Cazotte, writing in the early 1740s, should have moved rapidly from the light-hearted but relatively earnest *La Patte du chat* to the chaotic absurdity of *Les Mille et une fadaises*.

La Patte du chat, openly imitative of Thomas Gueullette's pastiches of Galland, describes the amazing adventures of the long-nosed Amadil, exiled from the country of Zimzim for treading on the paw of the queen's favorite cat (which turns out, in the end, to be an evil magician in disguise). *Les Mille et une fadaises* establishes its credentials by posing as a tale concocted by an abbé as a cure for the insomnia of two bored ladies of leisure. Its opening parodies the tale of the sleeping beauty, although the multiply

151

hunchbacked evil fairy is somewhat inconvenienced in delivering her curse by virtue of getting stuck in the chimney. Its penultimate sequence parodies the most celebrated of the licentious fairy tales, *Le Sopha* (1740) by Crébillon *fils*, in featuring a room entirely furnished by people magically transformed into appropriate pieces of furniture. The middle of the story is interrupted by an entirely irrelevant account of the adventures of a knight from the moon who has descended to earth by filling his head with ideas, thus rendering himself vulnerable to the force of gravity which is impotent to affect his light-minded fellow lunarians.

It is interesting to contrast these early tales, which are consciencelessly slapdash, with "La Belle par accident," a story of the same type first published nearly half a century afterwards. Here the hero Kallibad is an avatar of Don Quixote, deluded by overindulgence in the delights of fantastic fiction into an inability to separate fact from fancy, but Cazotte is far more forgiving than Cervantes had been and he is careful to excuse and endorse a moderate level of affection for fantasy.

Ollivier attempts to do for the chivalric romance what *La Patte du chat* had done for the fairy tale, but in order to do so it extends to a much greater length. Cazotte seems not to have been entirely comfortable with a project of this magnitude, probably because he was used to making up his plots as he went along, and the confused nature of the story owes more to lack of organization than calculated satire. The four subplots are untidily entwined, and the eventual *dénouement* is both anti-climatic and incomplete. If, as is sometime alleged, the model of the story was Ariosto's *Orlando Furioso*, the imitation is very pale indeed.

Just as he returned to the *conte de fées* in the latter part of his career, so Cazotte returned to the chivalric romance, with the much shorter "L'Honneur perdu et recouvré" (published 1788). The irony in this later tale is so muted as to be almost imperceptible, and it passed for a genuine example of the species—with the ironic result that it became popular with a wider readership than most of the author's other works.

Le Lord impromptu is a more interesting experiment than *Ollivier*, although it stands almost alone in Cazotte's oeuvre in having no supernatural elements. It masquerades as a translation from the English and its models are to be found among the less earnest of early English novels—it is closest in spirit to Fielding's parodies of Richardson, especially *Joseph Andrews* (1742). The story's hero, Richard O'Berthon, is raised as a gentleman and a scholar, but loses his income and is forced to seek employment as a servant. Thus misplaced within the class structure (a fate which he shares, of course, with the heroes and heroines of countless English domestic melodramas) he is inevitably drawn to commit the cardinal sin of falling in love with the daughter of the house in which he is employed. In the wake of a tragic misunderstanding he is forced to flee the vengeance of his employer, and spends the greater part of the plot disguised as a girl, under the protection of the enigmatic and resourceful Captain Sentry (who ultimately turns out to be his mother in male disguise).

The outsider's view of English manners and the *clichés* of English popular fiction which Cazotte lays out in *Le Lord impromptu* is understandably jaundiced, and it is not entirely surprising that in spite of its setting and subject-matter the novel was not translated into English until 1927. Few English commentators have had a kind word to say about the work, but it certainly demonstrates that Cazotte was not a one-book writer, and although the story is utterly incredible it is the most coherently-plotted of all his works.

* * * * * * *

Le Diable amoureux is by far the most original of Cazotte's works, taking fantastic fiction into fields which were then entirely fresh. The idea of erotic temptation was by no means new, the danger posed by demonic succubi having been included in the preaching of churchmen for several centuries, but that myth arose from and remained connected with erotic dreams. Although there is a point in *Le Diable amoureux* when Alvare wonders whether his entire adventure has been delusory there cannot possibly be any suggestion that it could all have been the dream of a single night. Although some of Alvare's adventures are written off as purely subjective experiences there is no doubt that Biondetta is real and that her attendance upon the hero extends over a long period.

Cazotte was later to say that the work as originally envisaged had two parts, the first describing Alvare's seduction and the second following his subsequent career as the devil's minion. He explained the non-publication of the second part (which, if it ever existed, has been lost) by saying that it was too dark to be welcomed by an audience in search of amusement and distraction. The removal of the second part was initially compounded by a softening of the ending of the first part; in the version presented in the first edition Biondetta does not complete her seduction but gives away her true nature by her calmness in the face of the storm, and is commanded to vanish—which she does, after briefly showing her true form for a second time. This abrupt conclusion proved unsatisfactory, however, and so Cazotte added (or perhaps restored) the episode of the farmhouse, in which Alvare finally yields to temptation.

This rewritten ending certainly provides a more interesting climax, but it also has the effect of significantly compromising the moralizing of the story. Alvare's mother, whose memory and image have functioned throughout the plot as a metaphorical guardian angel protecting Alvare against Biondetta's wiles is invoked as a savior, but it is not at all clear that Alvare's salvation from the consequences of his weakness is appropriate.

Had Cazotte stuck to his original plan, and let Alvare become a living servant of the devil, his story would appear very different to the modern reader; it would be an important prototype of Gothic fantasy. Indeed, insofar as *Le Diable amoureux* was influential upon the work of other writers it seems to have nourished Gothic writers rather more than writers in a lighter vein. Critics are uncertain as to whether it should be counted among the influences of Matthew Gregory Lewis's gaudy tale of horror, *The Monk* (1796), which features erotic temptation in a more lurid vein, but it seems not unlikely, given the fact that Lewis was sufficiently familiar with French work of the period to translate and then to write his own conclusion to Hamilton's *Four Facardins*. There is no doubt, though, that Cazotte was read and much admired by the most important German writers of terror tales, E. T. A. Hoffmann and Ludwig Tieck. In the form in which *Le Diable amoureux* has actually been handed down it is more closely related to a kind of fantasy which was to become much more openly sceptical of received ideas of good and evil, but the popularity of that kind of fantasy was not to become evident until the Gothic fad had run its course.

In the truncated tale with the revised ending Biondetta does the hero no lasting harm at all, and his romantic adventure with her might thus be counted (despite that it was not the author's intention) entirely to his credit. For this reason, *Le Diable amoureux* was eventually able to take its stand at the head of a tradition of overtly sceptical works which gradually muster more and more sympathy for the supposed agents of evil. It has clear thematic links with Théophile Gautier's "La Morte amoureuse" (1836; tr. as "The Dead Leman" and "Clarimonde"), whose title may well carry a deliberate echo, and with such stories by Anatole France as "Leslie Wood" (1892) and *La Révolte des anges* (1914; tr. as *The Revolt of the Angels*). In these stories the pleasure-denying morality of the Church is severely questioned, and ultimately condemned, and although that was not Cazotte's aim it is easy enough to believe that—like Milton, according to Blake—he was "of the devil's party without knowing it." The modern reader who follows Alvare's affair with the ever-obliging Biondetta can hardly help but find her charming even while refusing to be duped by the false explanation of her nature which she offers.

Ironically, if the imagery of Cazotte's tale lent inspiration to those who wanted to argue that the devil was not as black as the Church painted him, it also offered some inspiration for those who wanted to believe that all seductive women had a little of the devil in them. Baudelaire sometimes invoked Cazotte while lamenting his unhappy relationships with the opposite sex, and there is an echo of *Le Diable amoureux* in Barbey d'Aurevilly's collection *Les Diaboliques* (1874; tr. as *Weird Women* and *The She-Devils*).

It has to be admitted that the importance of Cazotte's tale is largely historical; so many tales of diabolical bargains have been published since 1772 that it cannot help but seem pale and hesitant by comparison with the best of them. Even so, it remains very readable, and it holds its essential fascination for anyone who can read it with an awareness of its context.

* * * * * * *

It would be premature to conclude this essay without mentioning an episode which has probably contributed more to Cazotte's posthumous celebrity than anything which he actually did or wrote: an oft-quoted prophecy which he is said to have issued early in 1788. This became famous enough to seem appropriate as the very first matter to come under consideration when Storm Jameson introduced the 1927 edition of *A Thousand and One Follies* and *His Most Unlooked-For Lordship*.

According to the story, Cazotte, whose reputation as a Martinist mystic was by then secure, told a sceptical gathering of the cream of the French intelligentsia—including the most celebrated of the philosophers of progress, the Marquis de Condorcet—exactly what fates would befall them in the coming years. Inevitably, so the story goes, these great men of the Age of Reason refused to believe that so many of them would die on the scaffold, or in prison; nor would they credit Cazotte's further insistence that the king and queen would be included among the victims of the coming Terror.

This prophecy has one important point in common with all great prophecies—which is to say that there is no record of it whatsoever in advance of the events which it supposedly foretold. Jean-François La Harpe, who claimed to have been present, left a very elaborate account of it in his papers, but this was not published until 1806, by which time La Harpe was dead and could not be questioned about it. One suspects, of course, that the gifts of hindsight might conceivably have been brought to the assistance of La Harpe's memory when he wrote his account; there is written evidence to supplement the conviction born of common sense, that La

Harpe intended his account as an allegory rather than a memoir (it is probably intended to dramatize the inconceivability, in 1788, of his post-Revolution conversion from free-thought to Catholicism). Needless to say, though, the prophecy has frequently been advanced as good evidence of the indubitable superhuman powers of the Illuminati and all who follow in their footsteps.

What the story of the supposed prophecy actually tells us is that the love-affair which the nobility of eighteenth century France had with the substance of fantasy was not quite the superficial dalliance that it seemed. The comedy and the burlesque, as always, masked real anxieties and touched upon deep-seated doubts. Even the greatest figures of the Enlightenment succumbed to the temptation to involve themselves with such literary confections (including Diderot and Voltaire—with whom Cazotte was acquainted and of whom he disapproved) and proved by their example that even the most frothy literary confections could be fully-loaded with caustic sarcasm.

Jacques Cazotte was not in the same intellectual league as Diderot and Voltaire, and this shows up in a comparison of their various fantastic fictions as well as in the fact that he eventually plumped for Mysticism instead of Reason. He was, however, a player of the same great game, which should by no means be written off as a trivial and insignificant amusement of no relevance to more serious affairs. As J. R. R. Tolkien has reminded us in his classic essay "On Fairy Tales," he whose imagination is too closely bound by the straitjacket of actuality cannot properly see where the bounds of Reason lie, and what the implications of Reason truly are. Unless we can understand nonsense we cannot clearly see sense; that is why works like *Le Diable amoureux* are important, not merely in the history of literature, but in the furnishing of intelligent minds.

SLAVES OF THE DEATH SPIDERS, BY BRIAN STABLEFORD

XIII.

THE TWO THOUSAND YEAR QUEST

George Viereck's Erotic Odyssey

My First Two Thousand Years: The Autobiography of the Wandering Jew was first published in 1928, rapidly achieving a *succès de scandale* which carried it through numerous reprints and created the opportunity for its two authors, George Sylvester Viereck and Paul Eldridge, to follow it up with two sequels: *Salome: The Wandering Jewess* (1930) and *The Invincible Adam* (1932). The books marked something of a watershed in the history of American fantasy, parading a flagrant eroticism which would not have been tolerated a few years earlier.

The much gentler eroticism of James Branch Cabell's *Jurgen*—expressed entirely in symbols—had caused much controversy in the USA in 1919, the year in which assertive American moralists won their greatest and most tragic victory in the form of the Volstead Act. With the demon drink supposedly banished the moral crusaders had quickly turned their attention to "pornography"; Cabell's book came conveniently—if rather absurdly—to hand and was swiftly banned in Boston. The ban did not, of course, work as intended; the publicity generated far greater sales than the book would otherwise have attained, wherever it was obtainable. It did, however, cause publishers to exercise an unduly sensitive discretion for the next ten years—a discretion which Cabell and his supporters resented very fiercely.

159

One of the effects of this phantom of prohibition on the US publishing industry was a kind of "speakeasy effect" by virtue of which much European fiction in an erotic/fantastic vein—including classic works by Anatole France and Théophile Gautier as well as more conscientiously erotic works by Pierre Louÿs, Rémy de Gourmont, Alfred Jarry, and Hanns Heinz Ewers—was reprinted in lavish illustrated editions "for subscribers only." These books came to constitute a kind of naughty library of works which were easily available to "connoisseurs" although they could not be found on the shelves of public libraries or general bookstores. The kind of fiction they contained was widely considered to be distinctly un-American, in that it was, for the most part, conscientiously decadent, not only in its breezy eroticism but in its frequent championship of pagan values against the moral oppressiveness of Christianity. This calculated paganism was most explicit in the urbane literary Satanism of France's *The Human Tragedy* (1895) and *The Revolt of the Angels* (1914), but is implicit in most of the works by the authors cited above.

The attack on Jurgen seems ridiculous today, in that the supposed obscenity of the offending passages is only evident to readers who can decode the symbolism, and may thus be deemed to exist entirely in the eye of the beholder. Even so, it expressed a widespread conviction that any dabbling in the kind of calculatedly-archaic and fondly fantastic material that Cabell favored posed a pollutant threat to the moral rectitude of a nation founded by valiant Puritans.

The few native American writers who had earlier taken inspiration from the lushly exotic kinds of fiction which flourished in the naughty library had found their endeavors unwelcome even at the bet of times. The fervor of Prohibitionism intensified that hostility, much as the trials of Oscar Wilde had earlier intensified moralistic hostility to those British writers who had taken aboard French notions of Decadence. Most American adherents of "Bohemianism" had already forsaken the cause—Edgar Saltus and James Huneker had directed their efforts in other directions while Lafcadio Hearn emigrated to Japan and Stuart Merrill elected to restrict his own endeavors to the French language—and it is hardly surprising that the roaring twenties saw the near-total eclipse of its ideologies. There still remained, however, a small group of immigrant writers who chafed bitterly under what they considered to be the oppressive narrowness of their adopted land's moral guardians, and raged intemperately against it. One of these was Ben Hecht, whose vividly offensive *Fantazius Mallare* was published ("for private circulation only") in 1922 with a blistering eight-page dedication "to my enemies." Hecht ended up writing for Hollywood, in a suitably cynical vein. Another was George Sylvester Viereck, who had come to the USA aged eleven in 1895; he followed a different but arguably parallel career path, becoming a journalist famed for his interviews with "great men."

Viereck's first "Bohemian" novel was *The House of the Vampire* (1907), a homoerotic tale of psychic vampirism seemingly inspired by Oscar Wilde's *The Picture of Dorian Gray*. The story describes the manner in which the genius—and eventually the consciousness—of a young writer is leeched away by an older and ominously versatile artist. This had been preceded by two earlier volumes, *A Game at Love and Other Plays* (1906) and *Nineveh and Other Poems* (1907), the former described by its publisher as treating "problems of life and love as seen through the medium of an extremely modern temperament." Alas, Viereck's temperament seemed altogether too modern to the American audience and his literary career did not develop as he would presumably have wished, although he published several more volumes of his own poetry as well as editing collections of poems by Swinburne, Oscar Wilde, and Lord Alfred Douglas. His reputation was not aided by his activities as an apologist for the German Empire during and after the Great War, but his ailing fortunes were spectacularly revived by the success of *My First Two Thousand Years*.

The window of opportunity though which *My First Two Thousand Years* passed had already been prised open by other writers, but very recently, and it still stood ajar as Viereck and Eldridge approached it. Cabell had, of course, remained active as a writer throughout the twenties, and—doubtless still pained by the injustice of the assault on *Jur-*

gen—had clung hard to his determination to oppose hypocrisy. His deft but cutting *Something About Eve* had appeared a year before Viereck and Eldridge's book in 1927. In the same year the satirist John Erskine published *Adam and Eve*, which carefully avoided any hint of literary Satanism but nevertheless trod on controversial ground in preferring the free-loving Lilith to the hectoring and hypocritical Eve. The humorist Thorne Smith had begun his long series of assaults upon the blindness of those who hated sex and strong liquor a year earlier, in *Topper*. It was, however, *My First Two Thousand Years* which shattered the barrier of primness which American publishers had erected, and left it in ruins.

* * * * * * *

My First Two Thousand Years displays a kind of jeering irreverence for the narrow minds of American Puritans which is closely akin to the dedication of Hecht's *Fantazius Mallare*. The story exhibits the same determined fascination with sexual psychology that Hecht displayed in that work and its sequel, *The Kingdom of Evil* (1924). A similar scientistic fascination came to preoccupy several subsequent writers in the same vein, including Guy Endore, author of *The Werewolf of Paris* (1933) and the remarkable Freudian romance *Methinks the Lady* (1945), and the early SF writer David H. Keller, author of the Satanist fantasy *The Devil and the Doctor* (1940) and the bizarre Freudian fantasy *The Eternal Conflict* (1949). Viereck had the advantage of knowing Freud personally—in the foreword to his last erotic fantasy *Gloria* (1952) he refers to him as "my friend and master, the Columbus of the Unconscious"—although it is not at all clear that Freud would have approved of the highly idiosyncratic use made of his ideas in *My First Two Thousand Years* and its sequels.

The plot of *My First Two Thousand Years* recounts the story of Isaac Laquedem, a Jew who rejects his cultural heritage by enlisting in the Roman army which occupied Judea in the time of Christ, adopting the name Cartaphilus to mask his origins. Cartaphilus knows Jesus personally but despises his prophetic ambitions, which he considers absurd. His hostility is increased when Jesus wins his dearest friends, John and Mary Magdalen, to the Messianic cause. Cartaphilus sees Jesus condemned by Pilate and follows him to Calvary, where he refuses an appeal for help after Jesus stumbles, thus occasioning the famous curse which secures his immortality.

In traditional extrapolations of the legend the Wandering Jew is a miserable figure whose guilt-laden immortality is horribly burdensome, but Viereck and Eldridge's Cartaphilus is far more resilient. He is in the prime of life and fully appreciates the wonderful opportunity which has been afforded him. He soon discovers that Jesus is not the only miracle-worker in the world, and deduces that Jesus's powers must have been natural, providing no evidential support for the delusion that he was the Son of God. Later, Cartaphilus concludes that his own condition is due to a spontaneous mutation of his flesh, for which Jesus merely provided a psychological stimulus. The problem of finding a purpose to guide him through a potentially-limitless existence causes him some slight anxiety, but he is in no mood to submit to "the Great God Ennui" without a fight and he embarks zestfully upon a twofold quest in search of wisdom and sexual fulfilment.

In pursuit of this quest Cartaphilus seeks out various sages whose bold experiments in thought and deed place them at the cutting edge of progress: a deliberately controversial selection which includes Apollonius of Tyana, Mung Ling, Spinoza, and the Satanist Gilles de Retz. The last-named attracts particular interest by virtue of his attempt to create a Homunculus, but he is cast as an out-and-out villain and is brought to ruin by Cartaphilus's design. Cartaphilus also searches for the secret of "unendurable pleasure indefinitely prolonged." He dallies with many women, but his attention is abruptly seized and gradually captivated—by means of a series of cunning temptations and frustrating evasions—by one in particular: an immortal woman who seems to him to be his destined partner in life. This female counterpart is the princess Salome, similarly condemned to immortality by Jokanaan (John the Baptist).

Throughout his adventures, Cartaphilus retains a determination to take his revenge on Jesus by smashing the Christian "empire of faith." This ambition leads him to be the secret inspiration of Attila, Muhammad, and Martin Luther. Their partial successes are, for him, steps on the path to a final conflict which he is in the process of engineering as the story proceeds towards the present day—which it does at a headlong rush, the last century figuring hardly at all.

Laquedem narrates this tale while under hypnosis, spilling it into the eager ears of two psychoanalytically-inclined scientists whom he meets while sheltering in a monastery on Mount Athos in 1917. They cannot agree as to whether the story is to be taken literally or figuratively, but they wholeheartedly endorse its significance as an allegory of humanity's progress to modern civilization. The final passages of the narrator's account of his adventures become rather surreal as he tells of his final rendezvous with Salome is a new Garden of Eden, where she is attempting to succeed where Gilles de Retz failed in creating an artificial human being. In accordance with her feminist principles this new being is to be a Homuncula rather than a Homunculus, capable of becoming the mother of a new and better race. Cartaphilus, meanwhile, has only one more phases of his grand plan to complete before he may join her again; he and his enigmatic servant Kotikokura are now in the process of unleashing the combined forces of a "Red King" (Lenin) and a "Black King" (Mussolini) upon the tottering "White King" which is Europe and Christendom, in order to clear the way for a Millennium very different from that imagined by the dutiful and misguided followers of Jesus.

The literary style of this narrative involves a curious alloy of the portentous and the comic, which may reflect to some extent the different agendas of its two writers (Viereck notes of the light-hearted and flippantly sarcastic *Gloria* that he had originally drafted it in a much more earnest mode, but had been persuaded to lighten it by the arguments of a young friend nicknamed "the Gadfly"). Had *My First Two Thousand Years* been one whit less witty and ironic than it is it might not have crept through the window of opportunity which opened before it, but there is no doubt that its lightness is a double bluff; the authors meant every shocking syllable of it, and then some. The success of the book allowed the collaborators to indulge their mocking fancies a little further in its sequels—which are more correctly reckoned counterparts, in that they run in parallel, only the final few pages carrying the story further forward in time—but they remained careful enough to fight shy of authentic literary Satanism. Their closest approach to that extreme is a mere flirtation, in a brief passage in which Cartaphilus and Salome improvize a fragmentary drama in which they take the parts of Lucifer and Lilith.

* * * * * * *

Salome is more overtly erotic than its predecessor, as befits an extrapolation of a tale beloved of so many famous Decadents—Gustave Moreau, Oscar Wilde, and Jules Laforgue all produced their own versions of it. Although Jokanaan declares that its sexy heroine is "too vile for the grave," the authors clearly do not agree.

Like the Wandering Jew's female partner in Eugène Sue's famous elaboration of the legend—who was Salome's stepmother, Herodias—Salome becomes symbolic of the plight of women in general, and the quest which gives her life meaning is the liberation of women from the curse under which the entire sex labors. While Cartaphilus attempts to inspire an endless series of anti-Christs Salome cleaves to those women fortunate enough to reach positions of political power, hoping to use them to advance the cause of feminism. With Queen Zenobia Salome attempts to resurrect the ghost of Cleopatra. In Africa—where Cartaphilus is worshipped as the god Ca-ta-pha by courtesy of the exploits of his "prophet" Kotikokura—she briefly establishes a religion of her own and tries to create a society where women are dominant. She is the creator of Pope Joan and Jeanne d'Arc and rallies to the causes of Elizabeth I of England and Catherine the Great of Russia. In every case, though, she is disappointed.

Perhaps inevitably, in a Freudian fantasy, it is accepted at the axiomatic level by Viereck and Eldridge that the exercise of power is essentially masculine. Salome discovers that powerful women can remain effective only while the process of their physical and psychological development is arrested; in the end, all of them become incompetent when they are weakened by the delayed onset of their "bloody sacrifice to the moon." Salome too is corrupted by nature, albeit more moderately, and she knows that she must eventually give way to the destiny which has marked her out as Cartaphilus's loving mate—but she cannot be content with that. If nature has made her frail, she is determined to overcome it.

Like Nietzsche, Salome looks forward avidly to the victory of the coming *Übermensch*—but unlike the misogynistically-inclined philosopher, she assumes that the coming regime will involve a new equality of male and female. In the novel, however, the World Spirit incarnate in Nature—as conceived and animated by Viereck and Eldridge—cannot yet tolerate such an evolution, and Homuncula is cataclysmically destroyed even as she is born. In the end, Cartaphilus has to console Salome with the proposition that the time is not yet ripe, and that there are preliminary dilemmas to be addressed and resolved as well as new scientific discoveries to be made before the human story can possibly reach that kind of climax.

Salome was almost as successful in the marketplace as its predecessor, and has continued to be reprinted along with it in various paperback editions, but the third volume in the series is not included in these more recent editions and failed ignominiously to achieve similar sales in its hardcover editions, perhaps because it is the most fantastic and most explicit of the three. *The Invincible Adam* is the story of Kotikokura, the servant and sometime worshipper of Cartaphilus, who began life as a proto-human but has evolved into a handsome person of culture and intelligence. In the first chapter we find him temporarily employing the alias Lord Kotesbury, on the run from the outraged forces of law and morality having allegedly molested a young woman. (The chase is interrupted by the declamations of an amateur philosopher crying "To Hell with Prohibition!"—the authors could not know that by 1937, the year in which the novel is set, the Volstead Act would have been repealed.)

Following his apprehension, Kotikokura defends himself before a jury of scientists, including those who earlier psychoanalysed Cartaphilus. He begins his tale with an account of his childhood in prehistoric Africa, when he was condemned to be sacrificed to his tribe's deity, the Great Ape, by virtue of possessing what the Great Ape has taken away from other men as a punishment: a penile bone. This is referred to throughout as a "rib," partly for reasons of coyness but mainly to insist that this equipment was what Jehovah took from Adam in order to make Eve. In the event, Kotikokura escapes his allotted fate, becoming instead an immortal heretic, devoted to the service of a new god, Ca-ta-pha, whose accidental (and wholly illusory) revelation gives him a purpose in life. This personal mission eventually reaches a kind of fulfilment when he meets the person who seems to be the incarnation of all his hopes and desires: Cartaphilus.

By virtue of his permanent erection Kotikokura is perennially popular among women even though he retains a crucial immaturity, having been made immortal when not yet fully grown. Although he seemed in the stories told in the first two volumes of the trilogy still to be primitive and simple-minded, *The Invincible Adam* reveals that this was mostly camouflage employed in his dealings with Cartaphilus and Salome, and that he is ready enough to display his sophistication to others. His physical appearance changes slowly with time, so that he "evolves" from being a dark-skinned pygmy to a condition in which he can pass readily enough for an English aristocrat.

Having heard Kotikokura's account of his irrepressible instincts, and the reason for the assault which he is supposed to have committed, the jury of scientists is prepared to concede that his occasional outbursts of erotic exuberance are entirely natural. His crime—biting the ear of the girl he is charged with molesting—is forgiven once it is explained that ear-biting was the ultimate gesture of affection in the tribe into which he was born, and still remains his ultimate tribute to female beauty. As in the first volume, the scientists cannot agree on the literal truth of what they have heard, but of its profound symbolic significance they have no doubt at all.

* * * * * * *

The Invincible Adam is followed by a "personal note" which explains the allegorical significance of the trilogy (somewhat after the fashion of Edward Bulwer-Lytton, who used to excuse his occasional ventures into fantasy by appending portentous allegorical decodings of a rather dubious nature). Kotikokura, this note assures the reader, "is the eternal youth—Pan, the Pied Piper, Michelangelo's David, David slaying Goliath." (As if this collection of analogues were not sufficiently bizarre, the authors subsequently add Gargantua and Til Eulenspiegel to it.) Kotikokura's ever-elusive goal is Love, which he can never attain because he is torn by a struggle within: "the struggle between the monkey and the god, the primitive and the sophisticate, subman and superman, the libido and civilization"—or, to put it another way, id and superego frozen in time at a point when they cannot quite be reconciled into a healthy ego.

According to this same scheme Cartaphilus is "the sophisticated, highly civilized modern man, conscious of the feminine component which he inherits from Mother Eve." He seeks "unendurable pleasure indefinitely prolonged and a new synthesis of woman." In so doing he becomes "brother to Faust and Don Juan" and also a kind of Everyman figure. Salome is his counterpart, "the sophisticated, highly civilized modern woman," free at long last of the seven symbolic veils which enshrouded her when she danced for Herod, but not from the burdensome restraints of her biological nature.

"Our saga," the authors claim, "aims to bridge the gulf between the sexes, to establish a truce in their ageless struggle," adding by way of justification that "The latest discoveries of endocrinology and psychology confirm the poetic intuitions of Plato. No understanding of love is possible until we realize that each sex bears within itself the replica of the other" and "No one can assail the inhibitions and complexes of life without attacking the taboos which dominate civilized man no less than his progenitor in the jungle."[1]

This note serves to emphasize the fact that the authors' intention to offend against the taboos of the censorious American tribe—and not to do the job by halves—has been backed all along by a genuine conviction that such taboos reakly do need to be smashed, in the name of Progress as well as that of Liberty. George Viereck's ideas about sex may have been decidedly unconventional but they were certainly sincere. His peculiar combination of prurience and eccentric feminism was to be given even freer rein in *Gloria*, in which a woman who might or might not be the Goddess of Love (a cynical character suggests that she is merely a deceptive drug-smuggler) insists that all the great lovers of history and legend were, in fact, woefully inadequate to the task of satisfying their female companions. According to her, Casanova—with the aid of a cunning technological device akin to Kotikokura's "rib"—was the only man who ever managed to overcome the limitations of male physique, and even he remained prey to the dismal faults of male psychology. As to the roots which this insistent conviction may have had within Viereck's own psyche we can, of course, only speculate.

As an extended *conte philosophique* Viereck and Eldridge's trilogy cannot hold a candle to Anatole France's fantasies, and as a exercise in eroticism it seems gauche when set beside the works of Pierre Louÿs. As Samuel Johnson famously remarked about a female preacher, however, the marvel is not that it is done well, but that it should be done at all. However blatant the trilogy's faults as a commentary on human psychology and human progress might be, the fact remains that it served as a powerful provocation to further speculation. It spearheaded a brief revivification of the tradition of American philosophical fantasy which had languished sadly since the days of Hawthorne and Poe, and which might conceivably have gone from strength to strength had not fantasy been condemned to the status of a mere genre—and consequently shunted downmarket into the pulp magazines—in the late thirties.

It is ironic, but not entirely inappropriate, that the influence of the Viereck and Eldridge trilogy should be most conspicuously exhibited by a work very obviously designed as a parody of it: *The Memoirs of Satan* (1932) by William Gerhardi and Brian Lunn. These British collaborators wholeheartedly—but very sarcastically—embraced the literary Satanism of which the two Americans fought shy, and were enabled thereby to adopt a rather more objective viewpoint than Viereck and Eldridge's all-too-human protagonists. The first part of the novel—which ends, in synopsis, by wondering whether Salome was an intellectual snob—is modestly entitled "My First 1,000,000,000,000,000,000,000,000,000,000 Years," and its subsequent sections expand upon the themes of the trilogy with considerable farcical effect. The book was not a great success commercially (parodies rarely are, for obvious reasons) but it remains very readable, and its satirical edge is unblunted by the passage of time.

The moral crusaders of America were able to wreak a revenge of sorts on George Viereck during World War II, when he was imprisoned for refusing to register as an agent of Germany—which he did on principled grounds, being no great admirer of Hitler even though he retained a patriotic fondness for the Fatherland itself. He died in 1962, aged seventy-eight; Eldridge—who was four years his junior—lived to the ripe old age of ninety-four. Their other work in collaboration was a conventional scientific romance in a decidedly British vein, *Prince Pax* (1933), in which the Ultimate Weapon is used to put an end to war. It was not published in America, which had no use for fantasies of that type until 1945.

XIV.

THE PROFESSION OF SCIENCE FICTION: 42

It is sometimes said that life begins at forty. Having recently passed that dubious landmark in my life I now feel that I am in a position to comment on this old saw. I find it on the one hand absurdly optimistic and on the other absurdly pessimistic. It is absurdly optimistic in making the bold assertion that one really can start afresh, discarding the legacy of the error-strewn past; it is absurdly pessimistic in tacitly assuming that everyone has to. Perhaps one might rather say, with apologies to George Orwell, that at forty everyone has the future that he deserves.

From one viewpoint, my entry into the profession of science fiction has been a recent one, occurring when I quit my job (abandoning as I did so any hope of ever getting another one) and became a full-time writer. From another viewpoint, however, this move looks uncomfortably like a mere capitulation with the inevitable—my final belated acceptance of a fate forged by a peculiar chain of petty obsessions and existential accidents.

I still, on occasion, bump into slight acquaintances to whom my defection from academic life comes as news. Some of them, exhibiting a flair for delicate diplomacy which is typically English, politely ask "Was that a brave decision?" I usually say yes, but it is a lie; I don't think that I have ever taken a brave decision in my life. In fact, I have difficulty in seeing the move as a "decision" at all; I see it rather as a matter of defaulting on my debt to society, or dropping out of the struggle to maintain a facade of respectability. It is an action perfectly consistent with the way I have contrived to live my whole life. In the human race I was always a long shot, destined to be listed among those who failed to win or place, but "also ran"; I sometimes feel that I should never have been entered.

* * * * * * *

Life actually begins somewhere around the age of four—at least, mine did. Some people claim to be able to remember a good deal about their infancy, but I cannot. I have written more than once that a good memory is one adept at forgetting, which does not clutter itself up with a crippling burden of trivia but concentrates instead on the important stuff. I always write this with a sense of self-satisfaction; its frequent repetition in my repertoire testifies to the fact that I believe myself to have a good memory. Unfortunately, I might be wrong. Perhaps I have actually forgotten all the important stuff and remembered only the trivia.

I can only take it on trust that the things I happen to remember are the things which were significant in forming my character. There are many people, I know, who would argue that I must have repressed all the vital and traumatic moments, and that I can never hope to understand myself unless I can delve into the mysterious depths of the unremembered to recover the truly important by some magical process of abreaction. If that is so, the bulk of what follows here is a waste of my time and the reader's. Freudians, Jungians and devotees of primal therapy might as well skip to the next article right away—but those with a less dogmatic interest in psychoanalysis may stick around, because I will permit myself the luxury of a little deep-psyche diving if and when it seems appropriate.

It seems to me now, looking back, that the experiences which truly shaped me, and set my steps upon the path which led me to what I am today, were those which happened to me between the ages of four and eighteen. I was no tabula rasa before that, and I hope that I have continued to gather knowledge and sophistication since, but the crucial blows of the sculptor's chisel—which eventually chipped away from the unhewn block everything that was not the science fiction writer—were probably struck during those years.

* * * * * * *

I had no sense of being a total misfit until I was four. The earliest sensations of being an outsider which my memory has preserved date from my first days at school (a hazardous *rite de passage* to which I came a little early). I am told that it proved very difficult to keep me in school during the first few days, because I kept returning home at breaktime, but I cannot remember why I did it. I do, however, recall several factors which exaggerated my sense of being apart from the society of my fellows.

I remained in the reception class of the school for only a few weeks before being moved up to the next grade; at the end of the year I skipped a grade entirely, so that at the age of six I was in a class of eight-year-olds. This was because I had already learned to read and do arithmetic before arriving, and the policy of the school was to move children along as ability dictated. There was, however, one subject for which I had to leave my advance class to return to the society of my peers: religious instruction.

The school was attached to a Catholic Church, and it took the business of indoctrination very seriously. The walls of all the classrooms were decorated with religious pictures; in art classes we colored in cartoons of the life of Jesus or painted pictures of Noah's Ark, and I can remember a history lesson we had one November 5th when we were told that it was wicked to attend bonfires because Guy Fawkes had been a good Catholic protesting against the iniquities of a Protestant tyrant. Despite this permeation of the whole world of the school by the True Faith, it was still necessary for me to be removed from my class of eight-year-olds and put back in with my peers because it was the six-year-olds who were rigorously prepared for their first Holy Communion, forced to rehearse the relevant ritual responses for both confession and communion. I loathed the indignity of that periodic removal, which I felt much more keenly as a proof of my separation and difference than the fact that I was normally taught in the company of older children.

I now assume that the humiliation of this experience might well have been responsible for the fact that I was already an atheist when I was hustled through that first communion, although there was never any question of my confessing the fact. I continued to attend church—and even, for a while, to receive religious instruction from my local parish priest—until I was in my teens, but although I never said so I never had the slightest doubt that the idea of God was utterly and absolutely preposterous. Every formal confession I ever made, from the age of six onwards, was completely false, and it never occurred to me to behave otherwise. I was able to contrive a total disconnection of inner belief from outward affirmation.

To this day, I have never been able to understand how anyone finds the concept of God remotely plausible. It seems to me to be a bizarrely ridiculous notion, and the fact that many people plainly do believe in a God is to me a fascinatingly inexplicable phenomenon. The further fact that some people have found and do find in that belief a sanction to commit the most appalling acts of violence and persecution, seems to me to be an awful tragedy; I am nowadays a very fervent and devout atheist, who considers that the hijacking of moral philosophy and moral teaching by religious men has been the worst disaster to have overcome mankind during the last eight or ten thousand years.

* * * * * * *

Among the several other factors which added to my sense of infant alienation, the most important was probably the fact that I developed severe myopia at the unusually early age of five.

The problems with my eyesight may or may not have been connected with a bout of the measles which I suffered. The conventional medical wisdom of the day advised that children bedridden with the measles should be kept in darkened rooms and not allowed to read—a rule which proved difficult to enforce in my case because I was already an enthisiastic reader and I keenly resented any attempt to curtail my reading.

My eyesight has continued to get worse throughout my life, although the rate of decline slowed as time went by. Whether any of this degeneration was really self-inflicted I do not know, but I do know that from the time of my first eye-test until I learned to be sceptical of all received wisdom I thought of myopia as something blameworthy, the result of my refusal to accept restraint while bedridden with the measles, compounded by continued wilful "straining." Throughout my childhood I was a very determined clandestine reader; I had a fixed bedtime until I was fifteen or so, and there was not a single night during my formative years when I did not read for two hours or more after being sent to bed. This usually involved leaving my bedroom door open so that I could read by the light of the electric bulb on the landing. It no more occurred to me to take any notice of my parents' instructions to refrain from reading and go to sleep than it occurred to me to take any notice of what my teachers said about God. I simply felt that I had to keep my after-bedtime reading a secret, and I did.

Because of my short-sightedness I was given spectacles at the age of five. I was the only child in my class with spectacles, so my classmates naturally called me "Speck"— which cognomen, although it was formed straightforwardly by abbreviating the commonplace "Specky Foureyes," had in my case an extra pertinence; I was small and thin even for my age, and my classmates were all two years older than I was.

It would be tedious to add further details to what is essentially an exercise in mawkish complaint. I am well aware that the sum of these incidents is woefully inadequate to excuse the fact that I have never felt any sense of belonging to the world in which I find myself, but I have no other excuse to offer. I have always felt myself to be an alien.

* * * * * * *

Psychoanalytic interlude: at the risk of being stupidly pretentious, I am tempted to suggest that the inexorable degeneration of my eyesight became a kind of personal metaphor for the whole process of my social isolation. Myopia blurred the entire perceived world so badly that almost nothing of it could be seen without the spectacles which were used in such derisory fashion to label me, and the social world seemed to become ever more elusive as that blurring got worse. The only activity which I could and did pursue without my spectacles was the activity of clandestine reading. Provided that I held my reading matter very close to my face I could still read without spectacles until I was about eighteen, and that was my habit—at least when I read in bed. The world of print remained present to my naked eye long after the world of objects had come to be contained in and contrived by the lenses of my spectacles.

I have always been prepared to say that books matter far more to me than anything else. I am aware that there is a certain silliness involved in trying to argue that the imaginary worlds entered via the decoding of texts could be more important than the real one, but that is the way I have always felt. I have always defined myself, labelled myself and entertained ambitions for myself entirely in terms of what I have read or will read, have written or will write, and have written or will write about what I have read or will read. This, more than anything else, is why the four-year-old hatchling that I once was had become by the age of eighteen the larva whose long pupation resulted in the imago which I now am: a writer (by profession), critic (by vocation) and social being (by aegrotat).

* * * * * * *

The science fiction part of it might have been an accident. Then again, it might not. Science fiction does have a certain special appeal to aliens. This is not so much because it is written by aliens, for aliens, about aliens—after all, virtually all works of fiction have that in common—but because it easily outdoes other genres in pandering to the wilder extremes of alienness.

In the early days of the SF pulps there were so few SF readers around that just being one could make you different from everyone else; mere possession of the habit was a rubber stamp certifying that you were authentically weird. By the 1950s that was no longer the case, and by the early 1960s the genre was overtaken by the tragedy of fashionability; by that time nothing less than total absorption was necessary to guarantee and sanctify full-blown weirdness—but the possibility was still there.

As Oscar Wilde (who knew what he was talking about) once observed, it is better to be beautiful than to be good, but it is better to be good than to be ugly—or to put it another way, it's better not to be weird, but if other people think you're weird anyway you might as well try to make a virtue of it by pretending that it's the way you want to be. The weirder they think you are, the harder you have to work in order to make weirdness appear virtuous. Science fiction helps, in several different ways.

One way in which science fiction helps is by being magnificently pretentious. All other kinds of fiction are straitjacketed by mundanity; science fiction has the infinite reaches of time and space to play with, and promises tantalising glimpses of a god's-eye-view from which everything else will seem reassuringly irrelevant. If you let science fiction set the standards for what fiction ought to be about, then all other fiction is about next-to-nothing.

Another way in which science fiction helps is by flattering the alienated ego in no uncertain terms. Science fiction is full of misunderstood supermen whose heroism is so deliciously unlimited that they can achieve apotheosis without benefit of divine intervention. At the end of the day Sherlock Holmes is only a junkie smartarse and James Bond is only a homicidal yuppie, but even the kids in A. E. van Vogt are destined to rule the Sevagram.

The infinite cunning of science fiction (although Americans, who tend to be addicts of all kinds of junk food, including material success, are sometimes too simple-minded to realize this) is that it can perform this flattering function even when it refuses such secular apotheoses, trading instead in lachrymose hopelessness. If alienation and despair are conditions of the universe, applicable to all possible beings and all possible projects, then we poor also-rans in the human race are merely sharing in the tragedy of universal mortality, and are in no way to blame for our own misery.

Science fiction also helps by presenting a series of characters who can be loved by those who are largely incapable of loving their fellow men. The alien isolated from his (or her) peers cannot really be expected to identify with the exploits of fictional persons whose projects and predicaments are defined largely in terms of social relationships. That fictions of the mundane variety describe a world to which the alien does not belong is immaterial; the point is that they describe a world from which he (or she) is actively trying to dissociate himself (or herself).

Science fiction frequently offers very different ideas of virtue, where success is not primarily defined as success in human relationships but as success in coping with hypothetical non-humans such as robots, the inhabitants of other worlds, and scientific problems. In Tom Godwin's classic "The Cold Equations," virtue resides in the act of chucking the girl out of the spaceship into hard vacuum, not in trying to form a meaningful relationship with her. No other genre of fiction can let your bitterest feelings off the hook as slickly and as satisfyingly as that, while simultaneously allowing you to be uninhibitedly sentimental about the likes of cute E.T.s and burbling robots.

* * * * * * *

I honestly don't know whether these ramblings include a correct explanation of the fascination for science fiction which I developed in 1962, when I was fourteen. I do remember that for most of the ten previous years I was aware of the existence of science fiction, but did not discriminate between stories of that kind and other kinds; I was a very voracious but utterly haphazard reader. After 1962, though, SF came to dominate my reading completely. For the next five years I read virtually nothing else.

Oddly enough, the first writer who ever made a deep impression on me—who really seemed to speak to me more intimately and more meaningfully than all the rest—was not an SF writer. I began reading him at thirteen, the age at which people traditionally begin to get hooked on SF, and he was the only non-SF writer whose books I continued to buy whenever I could find them in second-hand shops. The writer in question was P. C. Wren. At thirteen, I thought that *Beau Geste* was the best book ever written, closely followed by *Beau Sabreur, Beau Ideal, Spanish Maine,* and *The Wages of Virtue.* Later—in some cases much later—I managed to recapture an echo of the impact which those books made on me by reading others of his works, and there still, for me, is something uniquely fascinating about Wren's plot construction.

All the P. C. Wren books which so entranced me have one thing in common: they feature heroes who, as a result of some essentially decent, usually misconceived, and apparently trivial act, are set inexorably upon a road which will lead to dreadful suffering—from which salvation can only be won belatedly, if at all. Wren delights in presenting readers with images of heroes whose sense of duty moves them to acts of absurdly-exaggerated self-sacrifice. There is no other author who treats his heroic projections of himself so savagely; he is the literary self-torturer par excellence, and it is as difficult to understand why he put himself on that kind of rack so meticulously and so frequently as it is to understand why some readers find the process so fascinating to watch. Most people find his performances absurdly unconvincing, and viewed from an objective standpoint they undoubtedly are, but their effect on my thirteen-year-old self (and what remained of that self in subsequent editions of my psyche) has only been surpassed by a dozen or so works by other hands.

Looking back now, with the aid of a keener critical eye, I can see that Wren must have been a man eaten up by envious resentment. He writes about a code of virtuous behavior which was affirmed by the aristocracy (especially in its military institutions), but not actually observed by its proponents. His most memorable central characters are all on the fringes of the aristocratic world; they are outsiders permitted to look in but denied full membership. All of them fervently wish to be a part of the magical world of the aristocracy, but are barred by poverty or by descent from disapproved marriages. At the same time, all of them are perfect embodiments of the aristocratic code of virtue—a code whose standards the vast majority of the aristocratic in-crowd fails miserably to meet. Wren's "natural aristocrats," prevented from demonstrating their virtues in the conventional social and military arenas, do so instead in the least likely and least appropriate circumstances—usually in the French Foreign Legion—and this is presented to the reader as something very painful, deeply humiliating and utterly tragic. (One of the less fortunate aspects of Wren's work, his crude racism, is probably best understood as a logical extrapolation of this lunatic class-ism, as is much English racism.)

It hardly needs adding that there is a lot of science fiction which is similar to Wren's foreign legion fantasies in its emotional appeal—although very little of it labors under the handicap of being tied to an absurdly mythologized vision of the English class system. In SF versions of this kind of fervent morality play—which have been written in considerable quantities by Jack Williamson, A. E. van Vogt, Theodore Sturgeon and Philip K. Dick, to name but a few—the innocent protagonist is treated vilely by other human beings, who fail miserably to meet the standards implied by the word "humane," and must display his (or her) own finer nature by siding with (or actually becoming one of) the aliens, or the supermen, or the robots.

* * * * * * *

It was not at all difficult for me to mis-spend my youth utterly and completely in the avid consumption of science fiction. From the age of eleven I attended a single-sex school which was several miles away from where I lived—no other pupils of the school lived near me, and it was therefore difficult to extend any friendships which I formed there beyond school hours. My relationships with my schoolfellows, such as they were, were largely determined by the extent to which they shared my enthusiasm for science fiction. One who did—Craig Mackintosh—was sufficiently interested eventually to join in with experiments in writing SF.

180

SLAVES OF THE DEATH SPIDERS, BY BRIAN STABLEFORD

Writing is an essentially private business which certainly does not require to be done in collaboration, but the availability of a collaborator was of great importance to me. The chief advantage was that it provided motivation—it created a situation in which I had a responsibility to someone else actually to do what we had planned and agreed to do. That helped enormously to make the vital difference between abandoning work and seeing it through.

When Mack and I were fifteen we calculated that most paperbacks contained about 60,000 words. We planned a novel in eight chapters, each to be 8,000 words long, then divided the chapters up between us and wrote it. It took us about a month. We then divided the handwritten chapters between us for revision, but we never carried out the revision—mainly, I think, because the thought of trying to type out all those words was simply too daunting, given that we had no reason to believe that once we had a typescript we could actually sell the book.

Eighteen months later we wrote a novelette, grandiosely entitled "Beyond Time's Aegis" in much the same fashion. Because 10,000 words did not seem too long I actually managed to complete the task of revising it and preparing a submission copy in the space of a weekend. It wasn't easy for a one-finger typist, but when I had done it I felt a certain sense of achievement, and immediately sent it off to the editor of *Science-Fantasy*, to whom I had lately been submitting letters of comment. He bought it, and published it under the pseudonym Brian Craig.

I now understand how absurdly fortunate Mack and I were to sell that bizarre, episodic, plotless, and rather silly story. No doubt the editor saw in it certain seeds of promise, and he certainly had a keen desire to encourage new writers, but it was nevertheless a decision of astonishing generosity to accept it. The sale made a dramatic difference to my attitude to the possibility of being a writer. Mack and I wrote two more long stories in collaboration, neither of which sold, and I wrote dozens on my own, almost all of which were awful beyond belief, but the painful wounds inflicted by incessant rejection could henceforth only be superficial. I knew that acceptance was possible, and that possibility became the essential spur of motivation which drew me periodically back to the typewriter to peck out something new.

"Peck out" was, and remains, an appropriate description; I never did learn to type properly. Having taught myself to find all the keys with my right forefinger—save only for the shift key, which became the sole responsibility of my left forefinger—I never attempted to unlearn the technique in order to do it right.

* * * * * * *

The worst of the habits which I acquired in my early days as an aspiring SF writer was that of never throwing anything away. For many years I relentlessly cannibalized old manuscripts, borrowing descriptive passages and slices of action whenever there seemed to be an opportunity of putting them into a more promising story. This helped to give many of my early works an unfortunate patchwork quality.

One of the long stories which I had written with Mack—a 37,000-word short novel called "The Worlds Beyond the World"—told the story of a man trapped inside a curious fold in time, who catches glimpses of the entirety of future history. It had no plot to speak of, and unsurprisingly failed to sell, but the forty-odd glimpses of the future were to keep cropping up in my work for many years. A dozen or so were combined with an unsold solo novelette of the same period to form a makeshift first draft of *The Blind Worm*, which I stitched up and hastily revised in order to follow up my first novel sale. Half a dozen more were then built into the second half of another partially-drafted novel, *Watchgod's Cargo*, which ultimately appeared as *To Challenge Chaos*. Several more, including at least one which had already been re-used in *The Blind Worm*, were decanted into the visionary sequence in *Man in a Cage*. Others became the bases for short stories, including "The Prisoner in the Ice."

"Beyond Time's Aegis" did not escape this kind of reprocessing either; I rewrote it as the first half of a novel whose second half consisted of various bits of "The Worlds Beyond the World" and several short stories which had appeared in various fanzines (mostly in *Proteus*, which I briefly produced in collaboration with a fan named Tom Jones). That novel too proved unsaleable, although it has recently been published by the Borgo Press. Many of my other fanzine stories of the period were cannibalized for the visionary sequence in *Man in a Cage*.

I fear that I have never entirely shaken off this habit. I later expanded the other unsaleable novelette which I wrote with Mack into an unsaleable novel, which I hauled out of its file as recently as 1989 in order to borrow several of its key scenes for one of the pseudonymous novels which I was then writing for Games Workshop. There was a certain ironic propriety in so doing, given that I elected to adopt for Games Workshop the same pseudonym which Mack and I used twenty-five years before. I record all this now partly as the record of a curious folly, but also in case I should ever become an object of academic study—it might conceivably make a nightmarish jigsaw puzzle for some intrepid bibliographer.

* * * * * * *

I did not enjoy my schooldays at all. I was utterly incompetent in the matter of meeting the expectations which others had of me, whether the others in question were my teachers or my peers. This was not because of any rebellious streak or daring assertion of individuality—it really was simple and straightforward incompetence. I did not know how to organize my intellect in such a way as to cope with most of the everyday problems which presented themselves to me, and I had not the determination or power of perseverance to cultivate such organisational skills.

That incompetence, and the unhappiness which it generated, may not have been the only factors involved in my getting into science fiction, but they were the factors which determined the depth of my involvement: the sheer ravenousness of my appetite for it and the urge to create as well as feed upon it. Looking back now, I can see that no other fate was possible for me but that I should eventually be recruited to the profession of science fiction, and I cannot help feeling that it was only my general incompetence in coping with matters of life and ambition which delayed my final absorption for such a long time.

Because my birthday fell near the end of the academic year and because I was in a high-powered school I first sat A level examinations when I was sixteen. Whether my immaturity was responsible for my poor performance, or whether it was simply that I spent too much time reading science fiction and not enough time working I cannot tell—probably the latter, given that the diaries which I kept (in which there was nothing to record except for the books I read) revealed on later inspection that I read more than 600 SF books and magazines in 1964 and a further 600 in 1965. When the time came for me to resit the exams a year later I took the appalling step of giving up SF for two whole months—and when I went to university in October of the same year my reading habit became much more moderate. I only clocked up 450 books and magazines in 1966.

Those three years were of crucial importance in laying down the groundwork for my later career as a historian of science fiction. I systematically worked my way through the contents of the British Science Fiction Association's two lending libraries (in those days they had a magazine library as well as the book collection which is now housed at the SF Foundation). This process displayed to me both the pulp heritage of magazine SF and a good deal of relatively-obscure British scientific romance. I had not at that time the economic resources to be a collector—most of the material which I bought came from market stalls and was later traded in at the same stalls for credit—but my methodical borrowing ensured that when I did have money to spend in second-hand bookshops I knew what to look for, and how to recognize something interesting when I caught a glimpse of it. A little obsession can go a long way, if one is careful to capitalize upon it.

* * * * * * *

The University of York, to which I went in 1966 to study Biology, seemed to me to be the closest thing to Utopia which the world was likely to contain. For the first time

184

in my life I was able to meet members of the opposite sex, to make friends, and in general to have a social life. I was still utterly incompetent in all these spheres, but the environment was far more conducive to learning than any I had encountered before.

At university I was able to catch up (gradually) with all the vices from which I had previously been totally insulated. I took to gambling like a duck to water, and spent a great deal of my time as an undergraduate playing poker and backing horses. Drinking I took to far more cautiously, mainly because I hated the taste of beer, but after some years of practice I managed to develop a healthy appetite for wine. Smoking, fortunately, I had somehow contrived to try—and had heartily disliked—when I was thirteen, and I was never tempted to try again.

My most conspicuous vice—although I did not regard it as such at the time—was a penchant for bitter and scathing sarcasm which I had picked up at school. Having always been puny, I had channelled all my aggression into verbal warfare, and had become far too good at it. When I first realized how easy it is to hurt people with words I was delighted, because a society which consists entirely of teenage boys has norms of behavior that legitimize constant hostility— everyone must constantly strive to be as vilely vicious as he possibly can. When I moved into a different kind of society I thoughtlessly carried with me many habits which were entirely inappropriate, and it took me some years of real effort to set them aside, or at least to quieten them down to an acceptable level. One unfortunate thing about sarcasm, though, is that one never can lose a reputation for it—once people have the suspicion that you might be being sarcastic, even the most sincere and heartfelt compliment is likely to be perceived as having a dark double meaning.

I am nowadays a very meek, placid, and mild-mannered person. I mean no harm to anyone. Nevertheless, there are still occasions when the old reflexes are unexpectedly triggered, and I still retain a certain gift for verbal viciousness and deadly insult. This would not matter much were it confined to everyday social intercourse, but it is something which has occasionally overflowed into my critical writing, especially into hastily-penned book reviews written while the disappointment of the reading experience was still preying on my mind. I try to avoid it (with increasing success as time has gone by) but there are still times when the temptation of a cleverly-crafted sneer prove irresistible.

This fault in my character devastated my social relationships for several years even in Utopia, and still does some disservice to my professional relationships. It may have had an effect on the reception of some of my fiction—I have written a lot of stories which do not make sense (or, at least, do not carry the intended meaning) unless they are read in a sarcastic tone of voice; some readers do not notice this at all, and some who do find it rather annoying. I keep trying to give it up but I doubt that I will ever succeed completely. Alert readers may have noticed a certain unfortunate tendency to sarcasm even in this conscientiously earnest and objective account of my decent into the Dantean realms of the profession of science fiction.

* * * * * * *

Term-time at university was very busy, and my financial circumstances were so straitened that I had to get paying jobs during the long vacations. This meant that my attempts to write SF became confined to the two short (four-week) vacations. Even that time seemed to slip by all-too-easily, and although I started a couple of projects in the first eighteen months of my career as a student I finished nothing.

I decided, when only ten days of my second Easter vacation remained, that what I needed was discipline, and that I would force myself to complete a novel by establishing a quota of 5,000 words to be written each night (starting work at midnight), and not permitting myself to go to bed until the quota was finished.

To make things easy I used a very simple linear plot: chapter one provided the characters with a motive for undertaking a long journey, chapter ten described what happened when they got to their destination, and the eight intermediate chapters described their encounters with various odd environments and nasty monsters. I wrote it in longhand, then

paid one of the university secretaries to type it out for me
(which, being somewhat undersupplied with work, she contrived to do in her normal working hours in the space of a
fortnight).

I sent the novel, *Cradle of the Sun*, off to Anthony
Cheetham, an editor at Sphere Books who had recently written a short piece in the BSFA magazine *Vector* in which he
declared his intention to boost Sphere's SF list and asked for
advice from the fans. Nothing happened for several months,
until I wrote a polite letter inquiring as to what had become
of the manuscript. Cheetham then replied, saying that the
novel was unsuitable for the Sphere list, but that he was going to New York in the near future and might be able to sell
it for me there if I was willing to let him act as my agent. I
agreed, and he promptly sold it to Don Wollheim for the Ace
Double series, which was then on its last legs.

Had I been more idealistic I might have realized then
that the die was cast, and could have concentrated my mind
on the business of becoming a better writer, properly fit to
join the august ranks of the profession of science fiction. Unfortunately, I had not the least confidence in my ability to
make a decent living as a writer, and so I procrastinated. For
the next twenty years I tried to keep two career strategies
going side-by-side (to the inevitable detriment of both). That
twenty years now seems to me to have been largely wasted,
in that the books I produced were mostly written in a hurry
to fit into the temporal interstices of an academic career
which I always secretly regarded as a fraud.

Hurried production became the norm from day one. I
was in my final year as an undergraduate when I made my
first sale, and dared not neglect my academic work too much
lest I fail to qualify for three more years in Utopia as a postgraduate student.

I had 18,000 words in hand of the novel which ultimately became *To Challenge Chaos*, but it seemed easier to
cobble together *The Blind Worm* from pre-existing materials,
so I did that first. After I sold *The Blind Worm* to Don Wollheim, Anthony Cheetham suggested that the time was ripe to
obtain a multi-book contract. On being asked how I might go
about this, he suggested that I outline space opera versions of

the plots of the *Iliad* and the *Odyssey*, and call the result a trilogy. This I dutifully did, giving the result the high-flown title Dies Irae; the promised multi-book contract duly materialized, as if by magic.

I finished the first draft of *Watchgod's Cargo/To Challenge Chaos* while waiting for my examination results to be published, then spent the summer vacation producing a submission draft and writing the first two volumes of the trilogy. As with all my previous works I did longhand drafts at night (when there were no distractions) but had to do the typing by day so as to avoid driving my neighbors to distraction.

By the time my first novel was actually published, late in 1969, I had completed four more—although *Watchgod's Cargo* was rejected by all the publishers to whom my agent initially showed it.

* * * * * * *

My postgraduate career in Biology was devoted to an experiment in animal population dynamics. Almost all previous studies in animal population dynamics had been carried out in the wild, because the generation time of most animals does not lend itself to laboratory study. I was to work with *Tribolium confusum* (the confused flour beetle, so called only because it had previously been confused with *Tribolium castaneum*, not because of any character trait of its own), which had a generation time of thirty days. In order to get data on enough generations the experiment would have to last two and a half years, and I would have to count my experimental populations every seventy-two hours. In the meantime, I conducted a number of parallel experiments in which populations of *T. confusum* were in competition with *T. madens* (the black flour beetle, unconfusable with *confusum* even in its larval stage). I also tried to build a computer model which would ultimately be capable of reproducing, and thus helping to explain, my experimental results.

For some time this research seemed to be going awry, because my computer models always forecast that the beetle populations would stabilize; this contrasted with all previous experiments, in which the populations always oscillated. One

American doctoral student had even produced a mathematical model of such an oscillating population. Two years passed before I realized that my models were not incompetent, because my experimental populations ultimately did what the models said they should do and stabilized. The oscillations in the American experiments were thus revealed to be an artifact of their counting procedure, and the doctoral student who had published the oscillation-producing model had simply lied about it—I found that if one actually put his figures into a computer his hypothetical population stabilized too. Thus I discovered that some "real" science is fiction too.

I did not suffer a nervous breakdown in the course of my experiment, but I did get sick of the sight of flour beetles, and there came a time when the thought of spending the rest of my working life with them, according to the conventional logic of academic specialisation, became quite intolerable. I became so disenchanted, in fact, that I never did get around to writing up my experiments and submitting a thesis—which was a pity, in a way, because the results were really very interesting.

This fortuitous disenchantment might have prompted me to become a full-time SF professional in 1972, thus saving me a lot of time, but it coincided with the end of my early success, which had rapidly come to seem like a flash in the pan.

* * * * * * *

After completing Dies Irae I wrote a novel based on a novelette I had written some years earlier with Craig Mackintosh. Don Wollheim rejected it, on the grounds that it was sick and far too downbeat—and he also complained that the trilogy had turned out far more downbeat than the original outline had implied. His rejection letter suggested that I had had my "head bent and [my] ego inflated by the so-called New Wave" and should make strenuous efforts to get my act together. Ace was in financial difficulties anyway, and the payments due on publication of the early volumes of the trilogy were conspicuous by their non-appearance. Furthermore, Anthony Cheetham had lost interest in being a part-time agent, because it was a trivial enterprise contributing nothing to his ambition to be a millionaire superstar of the publishing world before he turned thirty (an ambition which he subsequently brought to spectacular fruition).

In the summer of 1970 I began to write *Man in a Cage*—a novel with which I was much more involved than I had ever been with my earlier action-adventure extravaganzas, and which took far longer. Progress was handicapped by the fact that I knew while I was writing it that Don Wollheim would hate it, because it embodied all the things he most deplored. I eventually finished the first draft in 1971 but did not begin preparing a submission draft. Two other projects which I started were also abandoned when I could not muster any faith at all in the prospect of their eventual publication. I did finish the novel version of "Beyond Time's Aegis," but only by virtue of regarding it as a purely personal mission—I knew that the book had no hope of selling.

By the summer of 1971 I was totally demoralized. Don Wollheim was, of course, absolutely right to say that what I needed to do was to get my act together and start writing for the market, putting the action-adventure back into my books and making sure the endings were upbeat. It seems ridiculous now to say that I could not do it—of course I could have done it—but at the time it really did seem that I was powerless. My personal life was plagued by the kind of agonies and crises which I really should have got out of the way in adolescence (or, even better, not bothered with at all) and my view of the world was so thoroughly jaundiced that I simply could not express myself in any other way than bitterly.

No light appeared at the end of the tunnel until my new agent, Janet Freer, told me that Don Wollheim had left Ace to set up his own company and was looking for material. He was now willing to take *Watchgod's Cargo*, which he had previously rejected, and was prepared to look at some new proposals. Gritting my teeth, I dusted off an old aborted story about a crashed space pilot, and wrote down the outline of a plot extrapolated from it, using all the *clichés* I could think of. Said plot might easily have been found in *Planet Stories*, and made vague promises about an upbeat ending. If it sold, I resolved, I would make a series out of it and thus keep myself in work for years. Don Wollheim duly bought it—and then I had to write it.

I composed *Halcyon Drift* in a rather peculiar state of mind. I was determined to produce a publishable book, but I still had a mental block which stood in the way of whole-hearted enthusiasm. As I set out, I decided that although I would deploy all the promised *clichés* I would do my best to subvert—or at least to pervert—every one. I further resolved that this would be the first ever space opera series in which the hero would not only never shoot anybody but would never even hit anybody (and, if invited to fight, would always politely decline to do it). Because of these strictures the hero/narrator, Grainger, became something of a clown—but at least he was unusual, and his cynical rhetoric had a certain sarcastic charm which ultimately seduced me into liking the book much more than I might have.

Don Wollheim liked *Halcyon Drift* well enough to commission two sequels, and promised that I could add further volumes to the series if all went well. My writing career seemed to be unsteadily afloat again. Cautiously, however, I decided that it would be best to conserve my other options; this, coupled with my reluctance to abandon Utopia for the Real World, led me to my apply to the Sociology Department to become a postgraduate there.

My original intention in converting to Sociology was to become a demographer, adapting my computer models for use in the description of human populations. Unfortunately, the department's demographer left shortly after my application was submitted, and I was offered the alternative of joining a one year postgraduate course leading to a B.Phil. I accepted, and found two parts of the course which were of particular interest—the part dealing with the philosophy of social science, which helped to develop my embryonic interest in the philosophy of science in general; and the part dealing with the sociology of literature.

I decided that I could pass myself off as a sociologist of literature, and set out to write a thesis on the Sociology of Science Fiction. Some chapters of this project were submitted for the B.Phil. before I re-registered for a doctorate, while the fairly prolific spinoff from my explorations ended up in such diverse places as *Foundation, Vector*, and *Amazing*.

* * * * * * *

By the end of 1972 my career (and, indeed, my life) seemed to have turned completely around. I got married in September 1973, by which time I had completed three of the five projected sequels to *Halcyon Drift*, and had managed to sell half a dozen short stories. I was also half way through a submission draft of *Man in a Cage*.

In the course of a rather makeshift honeymoon in London my agent and I hustled through a program of meetings with publishers which was—on the surface, at least—highly productive. J. M. Dent had bought British rights to my six-book series; Quartet, having failed to buy rights to the whole Dies Irae trilogy only because Ace had stupidly sold the first volume to a publisher of instant remainders, decided that they would commission a new trilogy; Anthony Cheetham, having recently set up Futura, asked me to write two non-fiction books for a projected line of popular B-format non-fiction titles; one was to be a history of science fiction, the other a layman's guide to the wonders of modern science.

Flushed with this success, I finished the final draft of *Man in a Cage* in a fortnight and hammered out *The Fenris Device* (the fifth Grainger book) in a further three weeks. Then I set out upon a program of intensive reading for the book on the history of SF.

Between January 1974 and May 1975 I wrote the sixth and last Grainger novel, the trilogy—collectively entitled Realms of Tartarus—which I had sold to Quartet, and the two books commissioned by Anthony Cheetham: a 135,000 history of SF entitled *Scientific Imagination in Literature*, and a 100,000-word popularisation-of-science book called *The Mysteries of Modern Science*. I also wrote a short fantasy novel for children. I was, briefly, a full-time writer, utterly committed to the profession—but it all went sadly awry.

Quartet folded after issuing the first part of the trilogy (which sold disastrously, possibly because no copies were distributed outside the London area), and no US publisher could be found for it. Dent decided that science fiction was not their sort of thing after all and got out, leaving the Grainger series incomplete in hardcover and fouling up the timing of the Pan paperbacks. Anthony Cheetham shelved plans for his line of popular non-fiction books, ultimately rejecting *Scientific Imagination in Literature* and selling on *The Mysteries of Modern Science* (without consulting me) to Routledge & Kegan Paul. RKP eventually published it—Heaven alone knows why—as an academic book, in which dubious guise it sold very badly and was rightly condemned by its reviewers for shallowness and unoriginality. The juvenile fantasy failed to sell.

This chain of disasters was ameliorated somewhat by my agent's success in selling translation rights to the Hooded Swan series and the Realms of Tartarus trilogy, and by the fact that DAW remained a safe market. I wrote a new novel for Don Wollheim, *The Mind Riders*, and submitted with it a proposal for a new six-book series, promising that this one would be rather more earnest than the last (whose subversions and perversions of pulp convention had ultimately begun to annoy him). Don gave me a contract for the first three books of the series, bailing me out of a situation which threatened to become financially desperate, given that I had lately acquired a new dependant in the shape of my son Leo.

While my unease was still acute, however, my wife spotted an ad in *The Guardian*; the University of Reading needed a temporary lecturer in the sociology of literature to replace a member of staff who was on sabbatical leave. I did not think I had any chance at all of getting the job, given that my first degree was in Biology, but I applied anyway. Fortunately, the head of the department, Stanislav Andreski, thought that a degree in Biology was worth more than a degree in Sociology, and was also of the entirely justifiable but daringly unconventional opinion that the only relevant qualification for teaching the sociology of literature was to be a published novelist. I got the job.

* * * * * * *

I could not regard the Reading job as anything more than a stopgap but I did try to use it as a launching-pad. I applied for twenty-three other academic jobs during the course of my year there, but I failed to get a single interview (there are not many people in British higher education as calculatedly unorthodox as Professor Andreski was). Knowing that my escape from the uncertainties of full-time writing had only been postponed, I set myself a punishing writing schedule. In the course of the year I produced the second and third books in the new series for Don Wollheim, revised *Scientific Imagination in Literature* for resubmission to other publishers, and wrote a new juvenile fantasy novel.

The latter parts of this schedule were completed under awkward circumstances. In order to save some money so that we could buy a house while I still had a salary (and was thus able to get a mortgage) my wife and I moved in with her parents—who lived in Swansea. During the final term of my teaching contract I travelled to Reading on Tuesday mornings and returned to Swansea on Thursday evenings, lodging for two nights with Dave and Hazel Langford. This proved surprisingly exhausting, but I did save enough for a deposit on a house, where I hoped that I would be able to pursue my somewhat-delayed career as a professional writer in reasonable comfort.

In order to supply myself with work for 1977 I had obtained a second three-book contract from DAW to complete the Daedalus series (and Don had also been persuaded to take the ill-fated *Realms of Tartarus*, although he insisted on doing it in a single volume instead of three). More importantly, though, I was co-opted by Peter Nicholls—who had published a number of my academic articles while he was editor of *Foundation*—to work on an encyclopedia of science fiction which was being packaged by Roxby Press; in the course of a little over a year I produced 133,000 words for it, obtaining some benefit, at last, from all the work I had put into *Scientific Imagination in Literature*—which failed to sell even in its second incarnation.

Before 1977 ended, though, yet another freak of chance consented to divert the course of my life. The man who taught philosophy of social science in the Sociology Department at Reading decided to emigrate to Australia, and I was invited by the acting Head of Department (Professor Andreski was away on sabbatical at the time) to apply for the post. The opportunity was too good to pass up. I got the job, and a mere nine months after rejoining the profession of science fiction I abandoned it yet again. I was, however, on a three year contract which might or might not be converted into a tenured post and I was not prepared to take it for granted that my contract would be renewed. Because I was reluctant to take on the much bigger mortgage that moving to Reading would have required I decided to commute again, on the same three-day-week basis as before.

I continued writing, but the strains of commuting made it very difficult to write anything other than short pieces during term time. Because I was financially cushioned by my job I decided that I would abandon series hackwork and endeavor to write books of a slightly more ambitious nature.

After finishing the last of the Daedalus books I outlined one such project—*The Walking Shadow*—and sold it in the UK to Fontana, who had just bought UK rights to *The Mind Riders*. I had two other projects to complete before I began work on it. The first was my long-delayed doctoral thesis, which I was strongly advised to write up in order to strengthen my case for being given tenure. The second was to prove the most disastrous episode in a career which already seemed to me to have had more than its fair share of ups-and-downs.

* * * * * * *

During my first year at Reading I had met the widow of the SF writer James Blish, about whom I had written a long article for *Foundation*'s special memorial issue. In the course of sorting out the Blish estate she ran into difficulties with Doubleday, who had commissioned Blish to write a history of witchcraft for them before he contracted the cancer which ultimately killed him; now that he was dead, they wanted their money ($6,500) back. Judy—who was not at that time certain that the estate could find the money—suggested that she look for someone who might complete the book. Doubleday agreed, but refused to pay out any more until the manuscript was in their hands. Judy asked me if I would do the book for the remainder of the advance plus a fee to be paid by the estate. I agreed, even though Blish had only managed to complete about 10,000 words of first draft and I would have to produce the book more-or-less from scratch.

Having researched the book for a year I spent the first half of 1978 producing a manuscript of some 120,000 words. When it went to Doubleday they replied—without even bothering to read it—that there had been a change of policy and that the company was no longer doing non-fiction for the mass-market; they had written off the $6,500 and were not prepared to honor the remade contract. I already knew before this happened that the ethics of the publishing industry were somewhat suspect, as one would expect in a profession consisting entirely of entrepreneurial middlemen, but this has always seemed to me to be despicable behavior.

The failure of the witchcraft book was compounded by the failure of *The Walking Shadow* to sell in America. Insult was added to injury when Fontana decided that they would abandon their SF line; in order to break even they printed only 12,500 copies of the book (which sold out instantly), and declined to reprint it. This did not seem to matter, because I was then taken on by Pan, who gave me a two-book contract and made encouraging noises about buying *Realms of Tartarus* if I could get Quartet to revert the rights. Quartet eventually did so, but only after representations from my solicitor. Unfortunately, they had delayed long enough for Pan to get into the same state as Fontana, forced by economic recession to abandon their SF line. Pan published the first of the two books they had commissioned but the second disappeared into a black hole.

Don Wollheim took the two books which I wrote for Pan and gave me a three-book contract for the initial volumes of yet another six-part series, but I was sufficiently chastened to decide that the state of the publishing industry made it imperative for me to continue my teaching career. When I was given tenure I decided that instead of producing the usual action-adventure hackwork I would follow my own inclinations and write a more contemplative book. Don rejected it, and told me to rewrite it with much more zip. He was entirely right in his evaluation, but the rejection nevertheless threw me into a state of utter dejection.

I could not face the thought of producing another series to order, so I asked Don Wollheim if he would take three separate books instead. He agreed, and I rapidly dashed off *Journey to the Centre* and *The Gates of Eden*, both of them obvious pastiches of my earlier series. Half way through the third such exercise in self-parody, however, I felt that I had had enough, and I asked Don in mid-1981 either to take *The Walking Shadow* or to tear up the third contract; he chose the latter course.

For the first time since I had started writing, I no longer had Don Wollheim to fall back on. Any prospect of renewing the relationship vanished when *Gates of Eden* appeared with the last two lines missing. Assuming that they had been censored in order to make the end look more positive I wrote an intemperately sarcastic letter to *Locus* advising would-be readers of the change—which annoyed Don extremely, because in fact he had only contrived to lose the last page of the manuscript, and had not realized that anything was missing.

Feeling that I had been utterly defeated by circumstance, I gave up writing fiction altogether; I decided that I would concentrate instead on my academic writing and on popular non-fiction.

* * * * * * *

The gradual acceptance of science fiction into the repertoire of American Academia ensured that a steady stream of reference books was produced in the late seventies and early eighties. The pay was poor, and became poorer as the population of academics eager to work for nothing steadily grew. Such work kept me fully occupied for several years, but the stream inevitably dried up. The library shelves filled up, sales of new projects dropped, and the money on offer became derisory. There was, however, further spinoff from the reference-book work.

Roxby Press, packagers of the Nicholls encyclopedia and *The Science in Science Fiction* (which Dave Langford and I were brought in to rescue when Peter Nicholls failed to meet his deadline), asked me to write a coffee-table book on the impact of biotechnology, which eventually appeared under the title *Future Man*; Shuckburgh-Reynolds, the packagers for whom I wrote most of the SF entries for *Novels and Novelists*—and who were later to package *The Science Fiction Source-Book*—asked me to write an imaginary history of the future. This eventually became *The Third Millennium*, with Dave Langford co-opted as collaborator to handle the hard-science parts of the extrapolation. In parallel with this work I painstakingly researched my academic magnum opus, a definitive study of the British tradition of speculative fiction. It was ultimately published as *Scientific Romance in Britain, 1890-1950*.

Working for packagers, as I quickly discovered, is even worse than working for publishers, which is quite bad enough. Packagers tend to think of themselves as the true originators of their books, and of writers as mere hirelings delegated to supply the boring black-and-white bit which occupies the space between the pictures. A packager will labor long and hard over the production of a glossy package to show to publishers—which may then take two or three years actually to find a buyer—but will then demand the rest of the text in double-quick time, and will butcher it as he sees fit.

Future Man, as published, bears little resemblance to the text which I submitted. *The Third Millennium* was ruthlessly reduced by some twenty thousand words, mostly by virtue of the rigorous excision of all the explanations. Packagers only want the lurid bits and the funny bits; intelligence and argumentative scrupulousness are to them embarrassing excesses to be furtively discarded. They will tolerate facts in reference books, because they cannot think of any legitimate reason for excluding them, but their true ambition in most of what they produce is to reduce popular nonfiction to the standards of tabloid journalism, in the faint hope that they might thereby catch the attention of people who do not normally read books.

The frustrations of working for packagers were to some extent compensated by the freedom to write *Scientific Romance in Britain* exactly as I wanted it. When I delivered it I put in an outline for a new project which seemed to me to have more commercial potential—a book entitled *Eroticism in Supernatural Literature*, based on a long article on that topic which I had written for the Salem Press *Survey of Modern Fantasy Literature*. I had also begun researching an exercise in the sociology of popular culture, dealing with the explosion of British paperback book publishing during the post-war paper shortage, tentatively entitled *The Vulgar Avant-Garde*. I had completed the first three chapters of the book on supernatural literature when the publishers told me that they had been unable to fix up a deal with a US publisher to distribute it in America, and that it could not be commercially viable without such a deal. I abandoned the book in disgust.

This was undoubtedly a fortunate turn of events, although I did not realize it until the time came when I could contemplate the sales figures for *Scientific Romance in Britain* (157 copies in the UK, not counting the remainders). I realized that there is very little point in writing books of such an esoteric nature—it's not so much that they don't make any money, but that hardly anybody wants to read them. Leaving aside the tenure-and-promotion games which waste so much American paper, academic work in the humanities is essentially a form of vanity publishing. As the present volume and its many companions testify, however, it is a kind of vanity publishing to which I remain addicted.

There remain several large-scale academic projects which I would have liked to tackle had I continued my academic career. All the extant books on the philosophy of biology are desperately bad, and virtually all books on the general philosophy of science concentrate far too much on building models based on the underlying logic of physics (within which biology cannot easily be accommodated). Then again, all the extant books on the psychology and sociology of gambling are either ludicrous or consist of extremely superficial surface-scratching, and I would have liked to put a wide-ranging study of psychological proba-

SLAVES OF THE DEATH SPIDERS, BY BRIAN STABLEFORD

bility into its proper context. No full-time professional writer could possibly consider wasting time on such projects, but in the unlikely event that I should ever become financially secure I would doubtless be tempted to look at them again.

* * * * * * *

Various factors combined to bring my writing to a complete halt early in 1985, for the first time in twenty years. My first wife had left me eighteen months before, arguing that there was no point in being married to someone as introverted, unsociable, and generally incompetent as me, and our divorce was then lurching through its concluding phases. I was deep in debt because of the divorce, and it seemed for a while that I would have to sell either my house or my book collection—a fate from which I was only saved by a couple of fortunate sales of translation rights to old works.

Late in 1986—after a gap of more than five years—I decided to have another go at writing fiction. The British market seemed to be booming again after a long period of stagnation, but at first I was carefully determined to take a hobbyist approach and I set out to write a number of short stories based on ideas I had been storing away for some time. I was greatly encouraged when the first two which I sent out were accepted immediately, one of them in America. My next eleven submissions to American magazines were all unsuccessful, but *Interzone* proved to be more hospitable and other markets were opening up in Britain. Furthermore, David Pringle—one of the editors of *Interzone*, with whom I had been acquainted for many years—was being asked for advice by various publishers keen to begin or resuscitate science fiction lines; his assistance proved invaluable in obtaining new contracts.

My morale was further boosted in 1987 when the International Association for the Fantastic in the Arts gave me an award for Distinguished Scholarship, and by an invitation to be one of the "keynote speakers" at a Symposium for Young Scientists and Engineers held in Tokyo, initiating a day's discussion on man's relationship with technology. In between the two events I remarried, and I suddenly felt far more cheerful and positive than I ever had before.

Fired by renewed enthusiasm I completed the first of two projected sequels to *Journey to the Centre*, which I had decided to turn into a trilogy in order to obtain belated British publication. Then I spent the greater part of the year working on *The Empire of Fear*, a long alternative history novel which was by far the most ambitious project I had ever taken on. This sold well enough to encourage its publishers, Simon & Schuster (UK) to offer me a three-book contract, and I was also offered a three-book contract by Games Workshop, who had hired David Pringle to head a publishing division marketing novels and anthologies of stories set in their various gaming scenarios. These two offers, added together, offered financial security for three or four years, and a chance—but no more than a chance—to establish a position in the marketplace secure enough to allow me to ride out the recession which would undoubtedly follow the current boom.

The timing of these offers was inordinately fortunate in coinciding with my progressive disenchantment with university teaching. The teaching itself I had always enjoyed, and the less pleasant aspects of the job—administration, marking, and so on—had never seemed particularly cumbersome. With every year that had passed since 1979, however, conditions had got steadily worse. The size of the department had shrunk by a third; it no longer had any postgraduate students, and there seemed to be a possibility that it might disappear altogether. The new Head of the Department reacted to these ominous circumstances by trying to make the course more appealing to students, gradually reducing those parts of it which were intellectually challenging. Because I was working on a word-processor at home I was very sharply aware of the many ways in which such a machine would make it easier to work in my office—which was not even supplied with a typewriter.

All these dissatisfactions were fairly minor, but given that I had abandoned academic writing as a bad job and that my fiction writing seemed to be going so well, the temptation to get out was simply too strong. It could not be justified

201

as a rational economic decision, but as a gamble it was simply too attractive for a man who was feeling more optimistic than ever before to pass up. I decided that I was old enough to do what I pleased, no matter what the risk.

* * * * * * *

I think that I am writing far better now than I ever did before. My years of writing criticism helped enormously to sharpen up my sense of what works and what doesn't, and I feel that I am at last competent to apply those lessons. The British SF market has now passed through its brief boom and is hurtling into deep recession again, but I am by no means as disheartened by that awareness as I once would have been. I am reasonably confident that there will be enough opportunities around to enable me to keep the wolf from the door, given that my needs are fairly simple. Perhaps more importantly, I now feel that I am doing what I want to do, and what I always did want to do even when I was terrified that I wasn't good enough to do it well.

I remain uncomfortably aware of the fact that many of the writers I hold in high esteem, whose prose and plotting seem to me to work best of all, died virtually penniless and deeply disappointed. No one can possibly have any right to expect better, given the worth of some of those who have already failed to make fortunes as SF professionals. Nevertheless, I must reiterate that my long-delayed decision to be a science fiction writer was not a brave one, and might as easily be seen as a cowardly act. The profession of science fiction is, after all, one which liberates its followers from the awful burden of confrontation with that sad, tawdry and frustrating riot of confusions which we call (rarely knowing how ironic we are being) Real Life.

I suppose that the rigors of natural selection must have adapted a few members of the human species for the ludicrous pantomimes of Real Life, but I am not one of them—and I cannot, in my heart of hearts, regret it. I would rather be what I am: an insignificant creature of strained sight and eccentric artifice, odd and alien and out of place. I prefer to dwell, for the most part, in a private world of cool cerebration where I am not required to sustain an intense and unrelenting involvement with the claustrophobic hive of human fears and affections.

* * * * * * *

Of course, this essay is all mere performance, with not an atom of authenticity in it—or so it seems to me. It is impossible for me to find any credibility in it even if I read it back to myself in a sarcastic tone of voice. Nor is there much in it which can really be of interest to anyone else, devoid as it is of plot or narrative drive or any sensible climax. Fortunately, there is no real need for me to try to explain myself, given that have I remembered and stated so confidently that every formal confession I have ever made, since the age of six, has been false. Even if one of them had been true, I know far better than to expect absolution from the sins which it recorded.

That is another thing which the profession of science fiction permits and encourages: ours is an art-form which attaches no value whatever to the truth; whatever is painstakingly descriptive of the actual is rightly deemed by the dedicated science fiction reader to be uninteresting (except, possibly, for such exotic follies of history as the French Foreign Legion).

I intend to spend the rest of my professional life telling lies, and will try as hard as I can to make them more credible than the dull and dire truth.

At forty, everyone has the future that he deserves.

NOTES

CHAPTER I

[1]Wilson, Colin. *Science Fiction as Existentialism*. Hayes, England: Bran's Head Books, 1978, p. 2.
[2]*Ibid.*, p. 4.
[3]Wilson, Colin. *The Occult*. London: Hodder & Stoughton, 1971, p. 10.
[4]*Ibid.*, p. 579.

CHAPTER II

[1]Atwood, Margaret. *The Handmaid's Tale*. London: Jonathan Cape, 1986, p. 144-145.

CHAPTER III

[1]Jones, Gwyneth. Letter in *Foundation* #41 (Winter 1987): 72-73.
[2]Le Fanu, Sarah. *In the Chinks of the World Machine*. London: The Women's Press, 1988, p. 186.
[3]*Ibid.*, p. 69.
[4]*Ibid.*, p. 176.
[5]*Ibid.*, p. 117.
[6]Livia, Anna. *Bulldozer Rising*. London: Onlywomen Press, 1988, p. 143.

CHAPTER IV

[1]Britton, David. *Reverbstorm* #4. Manchester, England: Savoy Books, 1995, p. 4-5 (not all the pages are numbered).

CHAPTER IX

[1]Wells, H. G. *The Discovery of the Future*. London: Unwin, 1902, p. 1-3.
[2]Wells, H. G. *The Shape of Things to Come*. London: Hutchinson, 1933, p. 428.
[3]Bell, Neil. *The Seventh Bowl*. 2nd ed. London, Collins, 1934, p. 67-68. (The first edition was issued under the pseudonym "Miles".)
[4]Wright, S. Fowler. *Power*. London: Jarrolds, 1933, p. 25.
[5]Houghton, Claude. *This Was Ivor Trent*. London: Heinemann, 1935, p.321-323.
[6]Stapledon, Olaf. *Star Maker*. London: Methuen, 1937, p. 333.
[7]Wells, H. G. *Mind at the End of Its Tether*. London: Heinemann, 1945, p. v.
[8]*Ibid.*, p. 17-19.

CHAPTER X

[1]Stoker, Bram. *Dracula*. London: William Rider, 1913 (tenth edition), p. 226-227. The "working papers" and sources used by Stoker during he composition of the novel are extensively reviewed in Part 5 of Christopher Frayling's anthology, *Vampyres: Lord Byron to Count Dracula*. London: Faber & Faber, 1991, p. 295-348.
[2]Leatherdale, Clive. *Dracula: The Novel and the Legend*. Wellingborough, England: The Aquarian Press, 1985; *The Origins of Dracula*. London: William Kimber, 1987.
[3]Florescu, Radu, and Raymond McNally. *Dracula: A Biography*. London: Robert Hale, 1973.

CHAPTER XIII

[1]Viereck, George Sylvester, and Paul Eldridge. *The Invincible Adam*. London: Duckworth, 1932, p. 411-412.

INDEX

Ace Books, 187, 189-190, 192
Acton, John, 32
Adam and Eve (Erskine), 162
Adams, Douglas, 7
"The Adventures of *Lord Horror* Across the Media Landscape" (Stableford), 5-6, 43-55
Allen, Grant, 105
All-Story Magazine, 133
Amazing, 192
Analog—SEE: *Astounding/Analog*
The Anatomy of Frustration (Wells), 107
Ancient Images (Campbell), 81-84, 92
Anderton, Constable James, 44-45, 47
Andreski, Stanislav, 193-195
"Angels, Plain and Coloured" (Wells), 98
Anno Dracula (Newman), 129
Anticipations of the Reaction of Mechanical and Human Progress upon Human Life and Thought (Wells), 95-119
Arabian Tales (*Continuation des mille et une nuits*; Cazotte), 148
Ariosto, Lodovico, 152
Arthur C. Clarke Award, 24, 26
"The Assassins" (Wilson), 17
Astounding/Analog, 9, 14
At the Earth's Core (Burroughs), 9
At Winter's End (Silverberg), 60-63
Atwood, Margaret, 5, 19-41
Bad Dreams (Newman), 91
Balcombe, Florence, 125-126
Barbusse, Henri, 13
Barrie, J. M., 142
baseball in fiction, 73-78
The Battle of Dorking (Chesney), 99
Battlefield Earth (Hubbard), 16
Baudelaire, Charles, 71, 155
Beau Geste (Wren), 179
Beau Ideal (Wren), 179
Beau Sabreur (Wren), 179
Beckett, Samuel, 13
"Beefsteak Club," 126
Bell, Neil, 108

"La Belle par accident" (Cazotte), 148, 152
Beresford, J. D., 105-106
Berkeley, Busby, 89
"Beyond Time's Aegis" (Mackintosh and Stableford as "Brian Craig"), 181-182, 190
Bishop, Michael, 6, 73-78
"Black as the Pit, from Pole to Pole" (Utley and Waldrop), 78
Blackwood's Magazine, 99
Blacula (film), 122
Blake, William, 68-69, 71, 155
The Blind Worm (Stableford), 182, 187
Blish, James, 195-196
Blish, Judy, 195-196
Bloch, Robert, 90
Blood and Roses (anth.), 131
Blood Games (Yarbro), 128
Blue Monday (New Order), 44, 49
Bogart, Humphrey, 88
"Bohemianism," 160-161
Bones of the Moon (Carroll), 84-85
Borgo Press, 183
Bosch, Hieronymus, 51
Boxtree Press, 92
"Bram Stoker's Dracula" (Stableford), 7
Bram Stoker's Dracula (film), 122
Brides of Dracula (film), 122
British Science Fiction Association, 184
Brittle Innings (Bishop), 6, 73-78
Britton, David, 5-6, 43-55
Brothers Grimm, 85
Browning, Tod, 122
Bruegel, Pieter, 51
Buffon, Comte du, 98
Bulldozer Rising (Livia), 28-30, 34-37, 40
Bulwer-Lytton, Edward, 167
Burroughs, Edgar Rice, 7, 9, 133-143
Butterworth, Michael, 43-44
Byronic fiction, 128-129, 131
Cabell, James Branch, 159-162
Cadillac Ranch (Springsteen), 44
Campbell, John W., Jr., 14
Campbell, Ramsey, 81-84, 86, 91
Camus, Albert, 13
"Carmilla" (Le Fanu), 125-126, 130
Carroll, Jonathan, 81, 84-86, 91-92
Carroll, Lewis, 27
Cartland, Barbara, 37
cartoons (film), 89-90

The Cave Girl (Burroughs), 142-143
Cazotte, Elisabeth, 149
Cazotte, Jacques, 145-157
Cervantes Saavedra, Miguel de, 152
Charnas, Suzy McKee, 33-34, 129
Cheetham, Anthony, 187, 189, 192-193
Chesney, George, 99
Chesterton, G. K., 116-117
A Child Across the Sky (Carroll), 81, 84-86, 92
"Christabel" (Coleridge), 130
"The Chronic Argonauts" (Wells), 98
Clamp, H. M. E., 142
"Clarimonde"—SEE: "The Dead Leman"
Clarke, Arthur C., 24, 26
Cohn, Nik, 43
"The Cold Equations" (Godwin), 178
Coleridge, Samuel Taylor, 130
Collins, Robert A., 6
Comeback Tour (Newman as "Yeovil"), 89
comic books, 6, 43-55
Condorcet, Marquis de, 156
contes de fées, 150-152
Contes de ma mere Loye—SEE: *Tales of Mother Goose*
Continuation des mille et une nuits—SEE: *Arabian Tales*
Coppola, Francis, 122
Corelli, Marie, 69, 71, 146
Corman, Roger, 89
Coulthart, John, 50-51
Countess Dracula (film)
Country Life, 36
Cradle of the Sun (Stableford), 187
Craig, Brian—SEE: Mackintosh, Craig and Stableford, Brian
The Cramps, 44, 49
Creation Press, 131
Crébillon, Claude Prosper Jolyot de, 152
Cumberbatch, Guy, 52, 53
Cutliffe Hyne, C. J., 105
Cuvier, Georges, 98
d'Aurevilly, Barbey, 155
The Dark Destroyers (Wellman), 9
"Dark Future" (series and game; Newman as "Yeovil" and Stewart), 89-90
Darwin, Charles, 103
DAW Books, 190, 193-194
de Gourmont, Rémy, 160
"The Dead Leman" ("La Morte amoureuse"; Gautier), 130, 155
Decadent Movement, 46, 51
Dedalus Press, 7

Defence of Poetry (Shelley), 145
Delany, Samuel R., 43
The Delta (Wilson)—SEE ALSO: *Spider World*, 17
Demon Download (Newman as "Yeovil"), 89-90
Dent—SEE: J. M. Dent
The Devil and the Doctor (Keller), 162
The Devil in Love (*Le Diable amoureux*; Cazotte), 7, 145-157
Le Diable amoureux—SEE: *The Devil in Love*
Les Diaboliques—SEE: *The She-Devils*
Dianetics, 14
Dick, Philip K., 180
Diderot, Denis, 148, 157
"Dies Irae" trilogy (Stableford), 188-189, 192
"The Discovery of the Future" (Wells), 95-119
Doctors Wear Scarlet (Raven), 130
Don Quixote (Cervantes), 152
Doubleday Publishers, 195-196
Douglas, Lord Alfred, 161
Downward to the Earth (Silverberg), 64
Doyle, Arthur Conan, 121-122
Drachenfels (Newman as "Yeovil"), 89
Dracula (Stoker), 7, 121-132
Dracula (film), 122
The Dracula Tape (Saberhagen), 128-129
Dracula's Daughter (film), 122
Dracula's Dog (film), 122
"Dracula's Guest" (Stoker), 121-122
Dracula's Widow (film), 122
"The Dream Bureau" (Wells), 98
Dream; or, The Simian Maid (Wright), 143
Dryden, John, 48
Dublin University Magazine, 126
Dune (Herbert), 59
Dying Inside (Silverberg), 64
dystopian fiction, 19-26, 34-35
Eldridge, Paul, 159-170
Elgin, Suzette Haden, 28
Elrod, P. N., 129
The Empire of Fear (Stableford), 129, 201
The Encyclopedia of Science Fiction (Nicholls), 194
Endore, Guy, 162
erotic fantasy, 159-170
Eroticism in Supernatural Literature (Stableford), 199
Erskine, John, 162
The Eternal Conflict (Keller), 162
The Eternal Lover (Burroughs), 142
The Evil Dead (film), 89
Ewers, Hanns Heinz, 160

existentialism in science fiction, 9-17
fairy tales, 151-152, 157
Fantazius Mallare (Hecht), 161-162
Farmer, Philip José, 141
Fascism, 45-47
Faulkner, William, 13
The Female Man (Russ), 34
"Feminism and SF" ("Forum" discussion), 41
feminism in science fiction, 19-41
The Fenris Device (Stableford), 192
"A Few More Crocodile Tears?" (Stableford), 5, 24-41
"Field of Broken Dreams: Michael Bishop's *Brittle Innings*" (Stableford), 73-78
Fielding, Henry, 153
"Filling in the Middle: Robert Silverberg's *The Queen of Springtime*" (Stableford), 57-65
film noir, 88
films in science fiction, 79-93
The First Men in the Moon (Wells), 97, 100
Fisher, Terence, 122
Flaubert, Gustave, 48-49, 51
Florescu, Radu, 127
Fontana Books, 195-196
The Food of the Gods and How It Came to Earth (Wells), 101
Forbes, Caroline, 33
Foundation, 5-7, 24, 27, 41, 192, 194-195
Four Facardins (*Les Quatre Facardins*; Hamilton), 151, 155
France, Anatole, 69, 71, 103, 155, 160, 169
Frankenstein (Shelley), 73-78, 123
Freer, Janet, 190
Freud, Sigmund, 142, 162
Futura Books, 192
Future Man (Stableford), 198
future war stories, 99, 101
futurism, 95-119
Galland, Antoine, 151
A Game at Love and Other Plays (Viereck), 161
Games Workshop (GW Books), 89, 183, 201
Garbageman (Cramps), 49
The Gas (Platt), 43
Gaskell, Jane, 130
Gates of Eden (Stableford), 197
Gautier, Théophile, 130, 155, 160
Gearhart, Sally Miller, 33-34
Gerhardi, William, 69, 169-170
Gilman, Charlotte Perkins, 33, 38
Gloag, John, 108
Gloria (Viereck), 164, 169

Godwin, Tom, 178
Gogol, Nikolai, 13
Gold Diggers of 1933 (film), 89
Gollancz Publishers, 99
"Grainger" series (Stableford), 192-193
Greene, Graham, 13
Greenland, Colin, 41
Greenwood Press, 6
Griffith, George, 105-106
Gueullette, Thomas, 151
Guidio, Kris, 44, 47-48, 50
GW Books, 89-91
"Gwyneth Jones: Weeping for Stableford," 24-41
"H. G. Wells and the Discovery of the Future" (Stableford), 6, 95-119
Halcyon Drift (Stableford), 191-192
Hamilton, Antoine, 151, 155
The Handmaid's Tale (Atwood), 5, 19-26
Happy Mondays, 49
Hard Core Horror (Britton), 47-49, 51, 53
Harrison, M. John, 43
Hawthone, Nathaniel, 169
Hearn, Lafcadio, 160
Hearst, William Randolph, 54
Hecht, Ben, 161-162
Herbert, Frank, 59
Herland (Gilman), 33, 38
Heseltine, Michael, 140
Hesse, Hermann, 13
His Most Unlooked-For Lordship (*Le Lord impromptu*; Cazotte), 148, 153, 156
Hitchcock, Alfred, 90
Hodgson, William Hope, 105-106
Hoffmann, E. T. A., 13, 155
The Holmes-Dracula File (Saberhagen), 121-122
"L'Honneur perdu et recouvré" (Cazotte), 152
"Hooded Swan" series (Stableford), 193
Horror of Dracula (film), 122
Hotel Transylvania (Yarbro), 128
Houghton, Claude, 109-111
The House of the Vampire (Viereck), 161
"Houston, Houston, Do You Read?" (Tiptree), 33
Hubbard, L. Ron, 9, 14, 16, 47
Huidobro, Vicente, 79, 81
The Human Tragedy (France), 160
Humphries, Judge Gerard, 47, 52-53
Huneker, James, 160
Huxley, Thomas Henry, 103
Iggy Pop, 49-50

Illuminati, 149, 157
In the Chinks of the World Machine: Feminism and Science Fiction (Lefanu), 28-30, 33-35, 40
Incarnate (Campbell), 82
"Intelligence on Mars" (Wells), 99
International Association for the Fantastic in the Arts, 200
International Conference on the Fantastic in the Arts, 57
Interview with the Vampire (Rice), 67-72, 129
Interzone, 7, 200
Invaders Plan (Hubbard), 9
The Invincible Adam (Viereck and Eldridge), 159, 166-168
The Invisible Man (Wells), 97, 100
Ionesco, Eugene, 49
Irving, Henry, 125-126, 131
"Is There No Balm in Gilead? The Woeful Prophecies of Margaret Atwood's *The Handmaid's Tale*" (Stableford), 5, 19-41
The Island of Captain Sparrow (Wright), 143
The Island of Dr. Moreau (Wells), 97, 99
J. M. Dent Publishers, 192-193
James, Edward, 5
James, M. R., 82, 84
Jameson, Storm, 156
Janson, Hank (*pseud.*), 52-53
Jarry, Alfred, 46, 160
Johnson, Samuel, 169
Jones, Gwyneth, 5, 24-41
Jones, Tom, 183
Joseph Andrews (Fielding), 153
Journey to the Centre (Stableford), 197, 201
Joyce, James, 48, 51
Joyce, William, 45-46, 48, 54
Jungle Book (Kipling), 142
Jungle Tales of Tarzan (Burroughs), 137
Jurgen (Cabell), 159-162
Kala (Luard), 135
Karloff, Boris, 81, 92
Kast, Pierre, 128
Keats, John, 130
Keller, David H., 162
The Kingdom of Evil (Hecht), 162
Kipling, Rudyard, 142
Koestler, Arthur, 73
Krokodil Tears (Newman as "Yeovil"), 89-90
la Croix, Mme., 149
La Fontaine, Jean de, 148
La Harpe, Jean-François, 156-157
Lady Chatterley's Lover (Lawrence), 36, 49
Laforgue, Jules, 165

The Lair of the White Worm (Stoker), 124
"Lamia" (Keats), 130
"The Land Ironclads" (Wells), 101
The Land of Laughs (Carroll), 84-85
The Land That Time Forgot (Burroughs), 135
Langford, Dave, 194, 197-198
Langford, Hazel, 194
Last and First Men (Stapledon), 109, 115
Last Exit to Brooklyn (Selby), 45
Latham, Robert, 6
Lawrence, D. H., 29, 36, 49
Le Fanu, J. Sheridan, 125-126, 130
Leatherdale, Clive, 127
Lee, Christopher, 122-123
Lefanu, Sarah, 28-30, 33-35, 40-41
Leinster, Murray, 9, 16
"Leslie Wood" (France), 155
Lewis, Matthew Gregory, 154-155
"The Limits of Individual Plasticity" (Wells), 99
Livia, Anna, 28-30, 34-37, 40
"The Living Dead" (Wilson), 17
Locus, 197
"London Fields" (Forbes), 33
"Lord Haw-Haw"—SEE: Joyce, William
Lord Horror (Britton), 5-6, 43-55
Le Lord impromptu—SEE: *His Most Unlooked-For Lordship*
Lord of Darkness (Silverberg), 59
The Lord of the Rings (Tolkien), 62
Lord of the Trees (Farmer), 141
Lord Valentine's Castle (Silverberg), 60
Louys, Pierre, 160, 169
Love and Mr Lewisham (Wells), 100
Lovecraft, H. P., 12-13
Luard, Nicholas, 135
Lucifer (Powys), 69
Lugosi, Bela, 81, 92, 122-123
Lunn, Brian, 69, 169-170
M97002 Hardcore (Proby), 50
Mackintosh, Craig "Mack," 180-183, 189
"Mad Planet" (Leinster), 9, 16
Madonna, 50, 127
"The Magic of the Movies" (Stableford), 6, 79-93
The Magician (Wilson)—SEE ALSO: *Spider World*, 17
Magill, Frank, 7
Man in a Cage (Stableford), 182-183, 190, 192
"The Man of the Year Million" (Wells), 98
"The Many Returns of Dracula" (Stableford), 7
Martinism, 149-150, 156

Marx, Karl, 31-32, 103
Masons, 149
Matthews, Jessie, 47, 51-52
Memnoch the Devil (Rice), 6, 67-72
The Memoirs of Satan (Gerhardi and Lunn), 69, 169-170
Men Like Gods (Wells), 101-102
Meng & Ecker (comic books; audio CDs, etc.), 6, 46-47, 49-51, 53
Merrill, Stuart, 160
Methinks the Lady (Endore), 162
Midnight Sun (Campbell), 82
Les Mille et une fadaises—SEE: *A Thousand and One Follies*
Mille et une Nuits (Galland), 151
Million: The Magazine About Popular Fiction, 7
Milton, John, 68-69, 155
Mind at the End of Its Tether (Wells), 112-114
The Mind Parasites (Wilson), 12
The Mind Riders (Stableford), 193, 195
Mirror of a Mage (film), 79
A Modern Utopia (Wells), 101-102
Modest Proposal (Swift), 22
The Monk (Lewis), 154-155
Monoshock (Guidio; Coulthart), 50
The Moon Maid (Burroughs), 135
Moorcock, Michael, 43, 52
More, Thomas, 38
Moreau, Gustave, 51, 165
"La Morte amoureuse"—SEE: "The Dead Leman"
Mosley, Oswald, 45, 47
Motherlines (Charnas), 33
motion pictures, 79-93, 122-123
"Mrs. Dale's Diary" (soap opera), 47
The Munsters (television), 123
Murnau, F. W., 122
My First Two Thousand Years: The Autobiography of the Wandering Jew (Viereck and Eldridge), 159-170
The Mysteries of Modern Science (Stableford), 192-193
The Nameless (Campbell), 82
The Napoleon of Notting Hill (Chesterton), 116-117
The National Observer, 98
Native Tongue (Elgin), 28
Nazism, 45-46, 54, 129
Necrofile, 6
The New Earth (Wilson)—SEE ALSO: *Spider World*, 17
New Order, 44, 49
The New Review, 98
"New Springtime" series (Silverberg), 65
New Wave, 189
New York Review of Science Fiction, 5

Newman, Kim, 81, 86-93, 129
Nicholls, Peter, 194, 197-198
Nietzsche, Friedrich Wilhelm, 166
The Night Mayor (Newman), 81, 86-92
Nineteen Eighty-Four (Orwell), 20-23, 25, 112
Nineveh and Other Poems (Viereck), 161
Nosferatu (film), 122
La Nouvelle Raméide (Cazotte), 148—SEE ALSO: *Rameau's Nephew*
Novels and Novelists, 198
Obscene Publications Act, 44, 49, 53
Obscene Publications Squad, 44-45
The Occult (Wilson), 12, 14
Oldman, Gary, 122
Ollivier (Cazotte), 148, 152-153
"On Fairy Tales" (Tolkien), 157
Onlywoman Press, 28-30
The Open Conspiracy (Wells), 102
Orlando Furioso (Ariosto), 152
Orwell, George, 20-23, 25, 112, 171
Other Dimensions, 6
The Outsider (Wilson), 12
The Palace (Yarbro), 128
The Pall Mall Gazette, 98
Pan Books, 193, 196
Paradise Lost (Milton), 68-69
Pasqualis, Martinez de, 149
La Patte du chat (Cazotte), 147, 151-152
The Penny Dreadful, 6
Perrault, Charles, 150-151
Peter and Wendy (Barrie), 142
Peter Pan (Barrie), 142
The Philosopher's Stone (Wilson), 12
The Picture of Dorian Gray (Wilde), 161
Piercy, Marge, 33
Planet Stories, 190
Platt, Charles, 43
The Plattner Story and Others (Wells), 100
Playboy, 38
Poe, Edgar Allan, 169
Polidori, John, 126, 131
Powys, John Cowper, 69
Primal Scream, 49
Prince Pax (Viereck and Eldridge), 170
A Princess of Mars (Burroughs), 135
Pringle, David, 7, 89, 200-201
"The Prisoner in the Ice" (Stableford), 182
Proby, P. J., 44-45, 49-50

"The Profession of Science Fiction, 42: A Long and Winding Road" (Stableford), 7-8, 171-203
Proteus, 182
Psycho (film), 90
The Purple Cloud (Shiel), 106
Quartet Publishers, 192-193, 196
Les Quatre Facardins—SEE: *Four Facardins*
The Queen of Springtime (Silverberg), 6, 57-65
"Rachel" (Cazotte), 148
Rameau, Jean-François, 148
Rameau's Nephew (*Le Neveu de Rameau*; Diderot), 148
Raven, Simon, 130
Raw Power (Iggy Pop), 49-50
Realms of Tartarus—SEE: "Realms of Tartarus" trilogy
"Realms of Tartarus" trilogy (Stableford), 192-194, 196
The Return of Tarzan (Burroughs), 133, 136-137, 142
Reverbstorm (Temple; Coulthart), 50-53
Revolt of the Angels (*La Révolte des anges*; France), 69, 155, 160
La Révolte des anges—SEE: *Revolt of the Angels*
Rice, Anne, 6, 67-72, 129
Rice, Elmer, 79
"Rice's Relapse: *Memnoch the Devil*" (Stableford), 67-72
Richardson, Samuel, 153
Robbe-Grillet, Alain, 13
Robertston, Q.C. Geoffrey, 52
Robinson, Edward G., 88
Rosicrucians, 149
Rousseau, Jean Jacques, 138-139, 147
"Route 666" (Newman as "Yeovil"), 89
Route 666 (ed. Pringle), 89
Routledge & Kegan Paul, 193
Roxby Press, 194, 197-198
Russ, Joanna, 33-35
Saberhagen, Fred, 121, 128-129
Sade, Marquis de, 13
Saint-Martin, Louis Claude de, 149
Salem Press, 7, 199
Salome: The Wandering Jewess (Viereck and Eldridge), 159, 165-170
Saltus, Edgar, 160
Sarraute, Nathalie, 13
The Saturday Review, 98-99
Savoy Books (and Comics), 43-45, 53-54
"A Savoy Deuteronomy Production," 48
Savoy Dreams (ed. Britton and Butterworth), 44
"A Savoy Gustave Flaubert Production," 48
"The Savoy Gustave Flaubert Salambo Orchestra," 49
"A Savoy Ionesco Psychodrama Production," 49
"The Savoy King Cocaine Band," 49

"A Savoy Parallax Production," 49
Savoy Records, 44-45, 49, 54
"Savoy Under Siege" A Report from Prison" (Britton), 44
"A Savoy Venus and Tannhauser Production," 48
Savoy Wars (CD), 50
"The Savoy-Hitler Youth Band," 44
Saxton, Josephine, 35
Schopenhauer, Arthur, 46
Schreck, Max, 122
Science Fiction & Fantasy Book Review Annual 1990 (ed. Collins & Latham), 6
The Science Fiction Source Book, 198
The Science Schools Journal, 98
Science-Fantasy, 181
Scientific Imagination in Literature (Stableford), 192-194
scientific romance, 99, 101-104, 107, 112, 115-116, 118
Scientific Romance in Britain, 1890-1950 (Stableford), 198-199
The Scientific Romances of H.G. Wells, 99, 102
Scientology, 14
Selby, Hubert, 45
Sesame Street (television), 123
The Shape of Things to Come (Wells), 101-102, 106-107
The She-Devils (*Les Diaboliques*; d'Aurevilly), 155
Shelley, Mary Wollstonecraft, 73-78, 123, 125
Shelley, Percy Bysshe, 145
"Sherlock Holmes" tales (Doyle), 121-122, 134
Shiel, M. P., 105-106
The Shiny Narrow Grin (Gaskell), 130
Shoot Yer Load (Meng & Ecker), 49
Shuckburgh-Reynolds, 198
Silverberg, Robert, 6, 57-65
The Simian Maid—SEE: *Dream; or, The Simian Maid*
Simon & Schuster, 201
"Slaves of the Death Spiders: Colin Wilson and Existentialist Science Fiction" (Stableford), 5, 9-17
The Sleeper Awakes (Wells), 101—SEE ALSO: *When the Sleeper Wakes*
Sleeping in Flame (Carroll), 84-85
Smith, Thorne, 162
Something About Eve (Cabell), 162
Son of Man (Silverberg), 64
The Son of Tarzan (Burroughs), 137, 139, 141
Le Sopha (Crébillon), 152
The Sorrows of Satan (Corelli), 69, 146
The Space Vampires (Wilson), 12
Spanish Maine (Wren), 179
Sphere Books, 187
Spider World: The Tower (Wilson), 5, 9-17
Springsteen, Bruce, 44

St. James Press, 17
Stableford, Brian, 5-8, 24-41, 129, 171-203, *passim*
Stableford, Leo, 7, 193
Stapledon, Olaf, 70, 108-109, 111-112, 115
Star Maker (Stapledon), 70, 111-112
Star Trek (television), 58
Star Wars (film), 9, 16, 58
Startling Stories, 15
Stewart, Alex, 89
Stoker, Bram, 7, 121-132
The Stolen Bacillus and Other Incidents (Wells), 100
Story, Jack Trevor, 43
The Strength to Dream: Literature and the Imagination (Wilson), 13
Strindberg, August, 13
Sturgeon, Theodore, 180
Sue, Eugene, 165
The Survey of Modern Fantasy Literature (ed. Magill), 7, 199
Swift, Jonathan, 22, 25
Swinburne, Algernon Charles, 161
"Sympathy for the Devil: Jacques Cazotte's *The Devil in Love*" (Stableford), 7, 145-157
The Tale of the Body Thief (Rice), 71
Tales of Mother Goose (*Contes de ma mere loye*; Perrault), 150
Tales of Space and Time (Wells), 100
Tarzan (film), 134
Tarzan Alive (Farmer), 141
Tarzan and the Ant Men (Burroughs), 134
Tarzan and the Forbidden City (Burroughs), 134
Tarzan and the Jewels of Opar (Burroughs), 140
Tarzan and the Lion Man (Burroughs), 134
Tarzan at the Earth's Core (Burroughs), 134
Tarzan of the Apes (Burroughs), 133-140, 143
Tarzan series (Burroughs), 7, 133-143
"The Tarzan Series" (Stableford), 7, 133-143
Tarzan the Terrible (Burroughs), 141
Tarzan the Untamed (Burroughs), 140-141
"Tarzan's Divided Self" (Stableford), 7, 133-143
Tarzan's Quest (Burroughs), 141
A Taste of Blood Wine (Warrington), 129
Temple, Paul, 50
Tempting Fate (Yarbro), 128-129
Things to Come, 101—SEE ALSO: *The Shape of Things to Come*
The Third Millennium (Stableford and Langford), 198
This Was Ivor Trent (Houghton), 109-111
Thompson, Bobby, 49-50
A Thousand and One Follies (*Les Mille et une fadaises*; Cazotte), 147, 151-152, 156
Tides of Lust (Delany), 43

Tieck, Ludwig, 155
The Time Machine (Wells), 6, 97-100, 114, 118
"The Time Traveller's Story" (Wells), 98
Tiptree, James, Jr., 33
To Challenge Chaos (Stableford), 182, 187-188, 190
Tolkien, J. R. R., 13, 62, 157
Topper (Smith), 162
Totem and Taboo (Freud), 142
The Tower—SEE: *Spider World*
Treece, Henry, 43
Twentieth-Century Science-Fiction Writers, 17
"The Two Thousand Year Quest: George Viereck's Erotic Odyssey"
    (Stableford), 7, 159-170
Ubu-roi (Jarry), 46
"Under the Moons of Mars"—SEE: *A Princess of Mars*
University of Reading, 193-195
University of York, 184-187
Utley, Steven, 78
Utopia (More), 38
Utopian fiction, 33-34, 38, 99-101, 103, 139
Vambery, Arminius, 126
"Vampire Chronicles" series (Rice), 67-72
"Vampire Files" series (Elrod), 129
The Vampire Tapestry (Charnas), 129
Vampires in fiction, 67-72, 121-132
The Vampires of Alfama (Kast), 128
"The Vampyre" (Polidori), 126
van Vogt, A. E., 12, 177, 180
Vector, 187, 192
Victorians, 127-128
Viereck, George Sylvester, 159-170
Viz, 53
Vlad Tepes, 126
Voice of Our Shadow (Carroll), 84
Volstead Act, 159, 166
Voltaire, François Marie Arouet, 67, 69-70, 157
A Voyage to Purilia (film), 79
The Vulgar Avant-Garde (Stableford), 199
The Wages of Virtue (Wren), 179
Waldrop, Howard, 78
Walk to the End of the World (Charnas), 34
The Walking Shadow (Stableford), 195-197
"The Walrus and the Carpenter" (Carroll), 27
The Wanderground (Gearhart), 33-34
The Wandering Jew—SEE: *My First Two Thousand Years*
The Wandering Jewess—SEE: *Salome*
The War in the Air (Wells), 101, 106
The War of the Worlds (Wells), 97, 99

Warrington, Freda, 129
Watchgod's Cargo—SEE: *To Challenge Chaos*
Weird Women—SEE: *The She-Devils*
Weishaupt, Adam, 149
Wellman, Manly Wade, 9
Wells, H. G., 6, 13, 95-119
The Werewolves of Paris (Endore), 162
When the Sleeper Wakes (Wells), 97, 100-101
Whileaway (Russ), 33
The White Stone (France), 103
Wild Cat (Clamp), 142
Wilde, Oscar, 13, 47, 125-126, 160-161, 165, 177
Williamson, Jack, 180
Wilson, Colin, 5, 9-17
Wollheim, Donald A. "Don," 187-191, 193-194, 196-197
Wolmark, Jenny, 41
Woman on the Edge of Time (Piercy), 33
The Women's Press, 28-30
The Wonderful Visit (Wells), 99
The Work, Wealth and Happiness of Mankind (Wells), 102
World Science Fiction Convention, 6
The World Set Free (Wells), 101, 106
"The Worlds Beyond the World" (Mackintosh and Stableford), 182
Wren, P. C., 179-180
Wright, S. Fowler, 108-109, 143
Yarbro, Chelsea Quinn, 128-129
Yeats, W. B., 13
"Yeovil, Jack"—SEE: Newman, Kim
"Yeovil" novels (Newman), 89-93
"Yesterday's Bestsellers" (Stableford), 7
Young Blood (Stableford), 129
Zola, Emile, 13
Zoltan-Hound of Dracula—SEE: *Dracula's Dog*

www.ingramcontent.com/pod-product-compliance
Lightning Source LLC
Chambersburg PA
CBHW031250090426
42742CB00007B/395